The Scie[illegible] Perf[illegible]mance

Keith Johnson

ISBN: 979-8-89212-324-2

Dedication

To every unsung athlete who tirelessly works behind the scenes, dreaming of reaching the stars, and to those who support them in their journey – this book is for you.

About The Author

Keith Johnson is not only a recognized movements specialist coach but also the CEO of North Star Sports. With an illustrious coaching career spanning institutions such as West Los Angeles College in 2024, East Los Angeles College, Glendale College, and Pasadena City College, Keith brings a wealth of experience to the sports coaching arena. His dedication to the advancement of athletes and his insight into the nuances of sports performance is exemplified in his new book, *The Science of Sports Performance*. With two decades at the helm of North Star Sports, Keith continues to inspire and shape the future of athletes.

Acknowledgment

First and foremost, my heartfelt gratitude goes to all the players and parents who entrusted me with their athletes and allowed me to utilize them in my research endeavors. Their belief and commitment to the process have been invaluable.

A special shoutout to Toledo Walls, the first player who ever approached me, seeking to enhance his performance. His journey, culminating in a national championship with Florida State as a walk-on, remains an inspiration.

I also want to acknowledge Jalya Figueras, a young man whose initial journey wasn't marked by the limelight. When he came to Glendale College, I was fortunate to assess and guide him. Through rigorous assessment and corrections, he exemplified the true spirit of a committed athlete. It's heartening to note his MVP win at the All-Star event, eventually earning him a scholarship from the University of Oregon.

Contents

Introduction

Sports-Specific Coaching Athletes today are constantly pushing their limits to achieve their desired level of performance. Whether it's in football, basketball, soccer, or any other sport, they strive to be the best in their field. As a movement specialist or coach, it's your responsibility to help them achieve their goals. One of the ways to do this is by providing sports-specific coaching.

Sports-specific coaching is essential for athletes who want to improve their performance. It involves tailoring training programs to the specific demands of a particular sport to help athletes develop the skills and fitness required to excel in their field. Sports-specific coaching is a specialized approach that takes into account the unique demands of the sport, the individual athlete's strengths and weaknesses, and their training goals.

Sports-specific coaching is especially important for athletes who want to compete at an elite level. In an increasingly competitive landscape, every edge counts, and sports-specific coaching can provide that edge. By focusing on the specific skills and fitness required for a particular sport, athletes can improve their performance and achieve their goals.

Benefits of Sports-Specific Coaching

Sports-specific coaching has become an increasingly popular approach to training for athletes across all levels and disciplines. This type of coaching involves tailoring training programs specifically to an athlete's sport, position, and individual needs. The benefits of sports-specific coaching are numerous and can help athletes reach their full potential both on and off the field. One of the primary benefits of sports-specific coaching is improved performance. By focusing on the specific movements, skills, and demands of a particular sport, coaches can help athletes develop the strength, speed, agility, and endurance they need to excel. This type of training also helps athletes refine their technique, which can translate into better performance and fewer injuries over time. Sports-specific coaching can also help athletes prevent and recover from injuries. By identifying and addressing areas of weakness or imbalance in an athlete's body, coaches can help reduce the risk of injury during training and competition. If an injury does occur, sports-specific coaching can also help with rehabilitation and getting the athlete back to full strength as quickly as possible.

Another benefit of sports-specific coaching is improved mental performance. This type of coaching can help athletes develop the mental toughness, focus, and confidence they need to perform at their best under pressure. Coaches can use techniques such as visualization, goal-setting, and positive self-talk to help athletes overcome mental barriers and stay motivated throughout their training. Sports-specific coaching can also have a positive impact on an athlete's overall health and well-being. By focusing on proper nutrition, hydration, and recovery, coaches can help athletes maintain their physical and mental health and avoid burnout or overtraining. In conclusion, sports-specific coaching can be an incredibly valuable tool for athletes looking to improve their performance and reach their full potential. Whether you're a coach, movement specialist, or athlete, incorporating sports-specific coaching into your training program can help you achieve your goals and stay healthy and motivated along the way.

Audience and Purpose of the Book

The audience for Sports-Specific Coaching for Elite Athletes is movement specialists and coaches who specialize in various areas of sports performance coaching, including strength and conditioning, endurance training, mental performance, nutrition, injury prevention and rehabilitation, speed and agility training, sports-specific coaching, youth sports performance, post-collegiate sports performance, and recovery and regeneration coaching. The purpose of this book is to provide coaches with a comprehensive guide on how to unlock the potential of elite athletes in football, basketball, soccer, and more. The book covers a range of topics, including the latest training techniques, injury prevention strategies, and mental performance strategies, all designed to help coaches improve the performance of their athletes. The book is also designed to provide coaches with the tools they need to help their athletes achieve their goals, whether that's winning a championship, breaking a personal record, or simply improving their overall performance. The book includes case studies and examples of successful coaching strategies, as well as practical tips and advice for coaches at all levels.

Whether you are a seasoned coach with years of experience or a new coach just starting out, Sports-Specific Coaching for Elite Athletes has something for everyone. From youth sports to professional athletes, this book is an essential resource for anyone looking to improve their coaching skills and help their athletes reach their full potential.

Sports Performance Coaching Principles of Sports Performance

Coaching Principles of Sports Performance Coaching Sports performance coaching is a multi-faceted field that involves several areas such as strength and conditioning, endurance training, mental performance, nutrition, injury prevention and rehabilitation, speed and agility training, sports-specific coaching, youth sports performance coaching, post-collegiate sports performance coaching, and recovery and regeneration coaching. To be an effective sports performance coach, you need to have a deep understanding of these areas and how they affect an athlete's performance. Here are some principles that can guide you in your sports performance coaching journey.

This impactful book reveals a new, advanced concept of preparing for sports competitions. Coaches do an excellent job of executing plays with precision, but at the end of the day, success comes down to the skill and speed at which players execute these plays. What makes specific plays and schemes work are athletes who can perform at elevated levels using the proper skill set and speed. When coaching, you must possess distinguishing ways to train and coach your athletes to perform at the highest level possible. Every player does not have the same skill level, so to be successful as a coach, you must be an effective communicator to reach your players—you need new communication skills to reach athletes today. If you only enlist one way of communicating, you will not be an effective communicator for your team, and you will not get the best out of your athletes. Coaches must assess their players' skillset and determine which skills and mental tools they need in the correct order to master their craft. I will also teach you how to access the mental and physiological foundation from which players come. Players' biomechanics must be observed and evaluated to determine which mechanics need improvements to increase performance. Understanding the angles is critical to developing an excellent athlete, and choosing which angles you need to correct is vital for optimum performance. It encompasses a mental program that is essential to becoming an extremely effective, high-level, winning coach.

You must understand and communicate with your players on a personal level so you can gain the highest efficiency from not only their physical skills but also their minds, which really work in perfect tandem when trained correctly. Several areas of CNS training are guaranteed to increase your athletes' performance. It's critical to regularly practice mental training with your players. Memory is not a memory stored in your muscles, of course, but memories stored in your brain that are much like a cache of frequently enacted tasks for your muscles. It is a form of procedural memory that can help you become excellent at something through repetition. Still, in precisely the same way, it can make you absolutely terrible at that same thing. Here is why: procedural memory and your brain can quickly instruct your muscles to carry it out. That memory does not judge whether you are doing good or bad, however, and so if you practice a song poorly for hours on end, you are going to be really good at making the same mistakes repeatedly. This is not only bad because you have wasted your time learning to be wrong or mediocre at a task and may see all this work as a failure but also because you did not necessarily have to fail at all. When you repeat mistakes repeatedly, you build memory with those mistakes. That makes those mistakes even harder to overcome later. This is one reason why the saying "you can't teach an old dog new tricks" is often true

KEITH JOHNSON

Chapter 1: How To Train The Reticular Activating System (RAS) To Increase Sports Performance?

Most sports training books will include a chapter on mental training somewhere near the back, after all the training exercises and drills and nutrition information. I put it first because an athlete can train all he wants to and be uber-talented, but if he lacks the proper mental training skills and mental arousal, he will not reach his full potential as an athlete.

Where is the reticular formation?

The reticular formation is found in the brainstem at the center of an area known as the tegmentum. The tegmentum is a heterogeneous section of neural tissue that extends vertically through the brainstem, making up the portion of the brainstem that sits between the ventricles and surface structures like the basal pons and the pyramids of the medulla. As the reticular formation is found at the tegmentum's core, it also runs along the length of the brainstem.

What is the reticular formation, and what does it do?

The reticular formation is a very diverse structure, containing various nuclei and numerous ascending and descending tracts. The fibers that traverse the reticular formation give the region a net-like appearance, which is where it gets its name (reticular means net-like). Due to the heterogeneity of the structure and the fact that there are no clear boundaries between the nuclei within the reticular formation, it was initially thought to lack organization.

However, it is now clear that the reticular formation is highly organized, just very intricate and complex. Among the numerous cell groups and tracts found throughout the reticular formation or connected to reticular formation neurons, some worth noting are nuclei involved in neurotransmitter production, nuclei associated with the cranial nerves, descending tracts involved in modulating sensory and motor functions, and ascending tracts integral to arousal and consciousness.

The reticular formation is home to several groups of cells that produce neurotransmitters. These neuronal populations have extensive connections throughout the central nervous system and are involved in regulating activity throughout the brain. One of the largest dopamine-producing areas in the brain, the ventral tegmental area, is in the reticular formation, as is the locus coeruleus, which is the most extensive collection of noradrenergic neurons in the brain. The primary sites of serotonin release in the brain, the raphe nuclei, are found near the midline of the brainstem in the reticular formation. The brain's largest areas of acetylcholine production, the pedunculopontine nucleus and laterodorsal tegmental nucleus, are found in the midbrain reticular formation. Neurotransmitters are produced in all these areas and sent throughout the central nervous system to modulate sensory perception, motor activity, and behavioral responses. Reticular formation neurons also form circuits with the motor nuclei of the cranial nerves; these nuclei contain neurons that are responsible for motor movements in the face and head, as well as motor movements related to autonomic functions of the visceral organs. Reticular formation circuitry helps to coordinate the activity of neurons in these cranial nerve nuclei and is thus involved in the regulation of simple motor behaviors.

For example, reticular formation neurons in the medulla facilitate motor activity associated with the vague nerve. This activity involves functions of the gastrointestinal system (e.g., swallowing, vomiting), respiratory functions (e.g., coughing, sneezing, breathing rhythm), and cardiovascular functions (e.g., maintenance of blood pressure). Reticular neurons in the medulla and pons also contribute to orofacial motor responses by coordinating activity in motor nuclei for the trigeminal, facial, and hypoglossal nerves. This activity, for example, allows for movements of the jaw, lips, and tongue that lead to the actions required for chewing and eating.

Reticular formation neurons are also important for facilitating the operation of muscles that allow for emotional facial expressions, like laughing or crying and coordinating eye movements. The reticular formation contains long ascending (i.e., traveling to the brain) and descending (i.e., spanning from the brain to the body) tracts. The descending projections are primarily involved with the modulation of sensory and motor pathways.

For example, projections extend from the raphe nuclei down to the dorsal horn of the spinal cord and can act to inhibit pain sensations. This is thought to be a significant component of descending pain control systems that allow us to suppress pain in certain situations (e.g., during a traumatic event). Other descending projections from the reticular formation are involved in the control of posture and movement. These fibers are mainly found in the reticulospinal tract, extending from the reticular formation to help maintain posture, facilitate stereotyped movements like stepping, and modulate muscle tone to either aid or inhibit activity. The reticular formation may be best known for its role in promoting arousal and consciousness.

The function is mediated by the reticular activating system (RAS), also known as the ascending arousal system. The reticular activating system contains circuits in several brainstem areas, including the midbrain reticular formation, ascending to the cerebral cortex and thalamus. These pathways are predominantly associated with the neurotransmitter acetylcholine and norepinephrine, which are thought to play essential roles in regulating arousal and wakefulness. The cholinergic neurons originate in the pedunculopontine nucleus and laterodorsally tegmental nucleus, while the noradrenergic neurons originate in the locus coeruleus. The fibers that arise from these locations combine with other pathways that ascend to the cerebral cortex and thalamus to promote wakefulness, vigilance, and overall arousal. These pathways from the reticular formation must be functional for normal attentional abilities and sleep-wake cycles to be preserved. Lesions to significant pathways of the reticular activating system can thus impair consciousness, and severe damage can cause coma or a persistent vegetative state.

Chapter 2: How does CNS training increase performance?

Training the central nervous system is essential for increasing athletic performance quickly, so as a highly efficient coach, you must understand how to teach the central nervous system through verbal communication and video training. I have used this technique for several years to train my players mentally to increase their performance. This is why you must be precise doing drills; each player must understand the drill verbally, not just visually.

The brain consists of four regions:

1. Cerebrum - the largest part of the brain and is responsible for higher-order functions such as thought, language, and emotions.
2. Cerebellum - coordinates muscles to allow precise movements.
3. Diencephalon – this region is located between the cerebellum and brainstem and acts as a relay station for incoming sensory nerve impulses, sending them on to the relevant areas of the brain for processing. The Diencephalon contains two structures:
   - Thalamus - keeps conditions inside your body constant, e.g., sleep, alertness, wakefulness, etc.

- Hypothalamus regulates your body temperature, hunger, fatigue, and metabolic processes.

4. Brainstem - the lowest part of the brain and is responsible for a variety of functions, including breathing, heart rate, and blood pressure.

From a coach's perspective, this is why we must do drills precisely in our warm-ups and in training to increase mental activity. So, exercises must be done correctly.

CNS Research

Research indicates that prolonged sports involvement influences the way the CNS 'controls' muscular recruitment and patterning. Researchers from Finland investigated the influence of sports background on leg muscle coordination during concentric and dropped vertical jumps. They discovered that the CNS influenced the firing and recruitment patterns of the sports participants' muscles. They attributed these differences to the specifics of individuals' sports and the effect years of training they had on the CNS. This is how you train the skill set to perform at a high level through technique. They went on to conclude that "Prolonged training in a specific sport will cause the central nervous system to program muscle coordination according to the demands of that sport" and also added, "the learned skill-reflex of the CNS seems to interfere in the performance of another task."

CNS training and 'quickness.'

There are two CNS processes related to sports performance – *excitation* and *inhibition.*

The speed at which signals are sent from the receptors to effectors and back again results in levels of excitation or inhibition. For example, to move the body as fast as possible when sprinting, the speed of signal transference through the CNS also needs to be as rapid as possible. An athlete's receptors and effectors, therefore, need to be optimally excited and uninhibited to result in the optimum recruitment of fast-twitch muscle fiber. However, CNS fatigue will slow the speed of excitation, particularly within fast-twitch fibers, which fatigue much more rapidly than slow-twitch fibers. Consequently, I believe exercises should only be performed as long as 'quickness' is possible.

Training the Central Nervous System?

Training the central nervous system is essential for quickly increasing athletic performance. As a highly efficient coach, you must teach the central nervous system through verbal communication and video training. I have used this technique for several years to train my players mentally to increase the performance of the CNS training system. This is why you must be precise when doing drills; each player must understand the drill verbally, not just visually. Receptor and effector organs: Receptor organs, which include the ears, eyes, and muscles, collect information (stimuli). The organs then interpret this information and send it back to 'effector' organs, which carry out the body's response to the stimuli. Some actions are largely automatic, such as the stretch and reflex involved in the leg muscles when being explosive, but others appear to be more interpreted by the brain.

Potentiation

Potentiation involves creating a set of stimulatory circumstances within the muscle firing complex that boost neural excitation, motor unit, and muscle fiber recruitment and reduce inhibition. Lifting weights before a plyometric workout (complex training) has been shown to enhance the performance of plyometric activity. However, any potentiating exercise must not fatigue the CNS; otherwise, the reverse effect will be experienced.

Weight Training

My philosophy regarding weight training to improve explosive power is that repetitions are the key training variable. I recommend a low number of repetitions (1 to 3), with loadings greater than 90% of 1RM, to develop strength that will boost speed and power and optimize the contribution of the CNS, with a recovery of 6 minutes between sets.

These loadings and recoveries are also recommended based on their contribution to maximum power and strength expression. These loadings create higher excitation and receptor/effector communication, more motor unit recruitment, and greater neural stimulation. They do not produce a large increase in muscle mass, which could be detrimental to an athlete's power-to-weight ratio.

Training planning advocates 48 hours of recovery between high-intensity CNS workouts. I also recommend that more of the same training be performed; this is partly because of potentiation and to create time so that the next day can be used for CNS recovery. For example, a sprinter could perform a sprint speed workout and equally intense plyometrics on the same day. On the subsequent training day, workout options would be selected to challenge the CNS, e.g., tempo runs (medium-paced runs that do not overly stress the anaerobic system). Consideration needs to be given to the training conducted in the preceding 24 hours.

Conclusion

Where speed and power are essential components in an event or sport, coaches and athletes need to plan CNS-specific sessions in their training programs. The training focus must be on the quality of execution (quickness) of an exercise, not the quantity. Over the past 20 years, I've called this neurological transmission something I studied in college. Electrical impulses sent from the brain transmit signals to your muscles to increase movement.

Chapter 3: How Does Mental Training Increase Performance?

Mental training involves the athlete imagining themselves in an environment performing a specific activity using their senses (sight, hearing, feeling, and smell). The images held in the athlete's mind should have the athlete perform successfully and feel satisfied.

What Can Mental Training Be Used For?

To familiarize the athlete with a competition site, a complex play pattern or routine, etc. Motivate the athlete by recalling images of their goals for that session, success in past competitions, or beating a competitor in the competition. Perfect skills or skill sequences the athlete is learning or refining. Reduce negative thoughts by focusing on positive outcomes. Refocus the athlete when the need arises; e.g., if performance is feeling sluggish, imagery of a previous best performance or previous best event focus can help get things back on track. See success where the athlete sees themselves performing skills correctly and achieving the desired outcomes.

Set the stage for the performance with a complete mental run-through of the critical elements of their performance to set the athlete's desired pre-competition feelings and focus.

When should mental imagery be used?

To become proficient in the use of imagery, you must use it every day: on your way to training, during training, and after exercise. Before you execute any skill or combination of skills in every training session, first do it in imagery. See, feel, and experience yourself moving through the actions in your mind as you would like them to unfold. In a competitive situation, use imagery before the event starts and see yourself performing successfully/winning.

How can I stay focused?

You have probably seen an athlete become angry at their performance. The situation here is that the athlete is focusing on the mistake (negative attitude), something that cannot be changed, and not on how to improve their performance (positive attitude).

I will talk about sports psychology 'pattern breaking' routines that help prevent the athlete from falling into a negative attitude. A 'pattern breaker' can be a word or phrase the coach uses in training or competition to move the athlete from a negative mindset to a positive one. Many athletes have a role model they try to emulate. Providing the role model is suitable; their name could become the pattern breaker phrase for the coach when the athlete takes on a negative attitude to a task. On hearing their role model's name, the mental arousal focuses on how their role model would react and assume a positive attitude toward the task. Over time, the mental arousal begins to recognize when they are focusing on negative thoughts and use the pattern-breaking word or phrase (repeating it in their head) to get themselves to switch off the negative thoughts and get back into a positive attitude.

What are the benefits?

Mental training itself can be helpful in several circumstances, including developing self-confidence and developing pre-competition and competition strategies that teach athletes to cope with new situations before they actually encounter them, helping the athlete to focus their attention or concentrate on a particular skill they are trying to learn or develop. When combined with relaxation, the competitive situation is helpful in the promotion of rest, recovery, and healing by removing stress-related reactions, e.g., muscular tension, establishing a physical and mental state that has increased receptivity to positive mental imagery, and selecting an appropriate level of physical and mental arousal before a competition.

A 14-week study of specific imagery and autogenic relaxation combined with standard physical training on football skill performance in novice boys aged 10–

12 years. The research revealed that "mental practice is effective for the preparation of the action. Furthermore, learning instructions on the movement effect related to the movement technique is more effective than learning instructions on a more distant effect. The present study results may have important implications for optimizing instructions for motor performance and motor learning in young athletes.

The "Quick Set" Routine

Psychologist Jeff Simons developed a routine that would allow an athlete to achieve appropriate mental arousal in the last 30 seconds before a competition. The "Quick Set" routine, which involves physical, emotional, and focus cues, can also be used as a means of quickly refocusing following a distraction. An example of this Quickset routine for an athlete could be: close your eyes, clear your mind, and maintain deep rhythmical breathing, in through your nose and out through your mouth (physical cue), imagine a previous race win, see yourself crossing the line in the first place, and recreate those emotional feelings of success (emotional cue).

"You only achieve what you believe."

I use this quotation when I hear an athlete make a negative statement about their ability and want to focus their attention when assisting them in developing mental imagery skills.

Coaching Point

The benefits of mental training have been outlined, and I have found that when an athlete is in a fully relaxed state, they are particularly receptive to mental activity.

The next stage is the creation of scripts to help in developing and applying mental training skills.

Conclusion

I will tell you a story about me as a young man. I was playing basketball one day with a man named Mike Ballou, who said, "You are a pretty good athlete. You probably could go to college if you worked at it."

It changed my life. It gave me the mental imagery of going to college and playing sports. It is also described as a verbal description of being positive, so mental imagery can be verbal, and mental training can be as simple as saying something positive. I have done this several times because someone else has done it for me. To make a long story short, the young man went to Florida State and won a national championship with Bobby Bowden. Toledo came up and said, I want to go to Florida State. I said, "OK, do me a favor. You get the academics, and I will help you get ready to make the team physically on the field."

So, I know that you can change kids' lives by giving

them positive mental instructions. This is why it's so important for coaches to have effective communication skills.

Chapter 4: How to transfer learning

The Learning Phases: Fitts & Posner Fitts and Posner (1967) suggested that the learning process is sequential and that we move through specific phases as we learn. There are three stages to learning a new skill.

1. Cognitive phase - identification and development of the component parts of the skill. It involves the formation of a mental picture of the skill.
2. Associative phase - linking the component parts into a smooth action. It involves practicing the skill and using feedback to perfect it.
3. Autonomous phase - Developing the learned skill so that it becomes automatic. It involves little or no conscious thought or attention while performing the skill. Not all performers reach this stage. The learning of physical skills requires the relevant movements to be assembled, component by component, using feedback to shape and polish them into a smooth action. Rehearsal of the skill must be done regularly and correctly.

Schmidt's theory (Schmidt 1975) was based on the view that actions are not stored; rather, we refer to abstract relationships or rules about movement. Schmidt's schema is based on the theory that every time an activity is conducted, four pieces of information are gathered: the initial conditions, i.e., a starting point, certain aspects of the motor action, how fast and how high the results of the action were, success or failure, i.e., the sensory consequences of the action—how it felt. Relationships between these items of information are used to construct a recall schema and a recognition schema. The Recall schema is based on initial conditions and results and is used to generate a motor program to address a new goal. The recognition schema is based on sensory actions and the outcome.

Adam's Closed Loop Theory Adam's theory (Adams 1971) has two elements:

- Perceptual trace: a reference model acquired through practice.
- Memory trace: responsible for initiating the movement.

The key feature of this theory is the role of feedback. Analyze the reference model's actions, the result of those actions, and the desired goals.

Transfer of learning

Galligan (2000) suggests that the transfer of learning can take place in the following ways:

- Skill to skill - this is where a skill developed in one sport influences a skill in another sport. If the influence is on a new skill being developed, then this is said to be proactive, and if the impact is on a previously learned skill, then this is said to be retroactive.

- Theory to practice: the transfer of theoretical skills into practice
- Training to competition: the transfer of skills developed in training into the competition situation.

Effects of transfer of learning

Galligan (2000) suggests that the effects of transfer can be:

- Negative— where a skill developed in one sport hinders the performance of a skill in another sport.
- Zero— where a skill in one sport has no impact on the learning of a new sport.
- Positive— where a skill developed in one sport helps the performance of a skill in another sport.
- Direct– where a skill can be taken directly from one sport to another bilateral transfer of skill from one side of the body to the other - use left and right.
- Unequal– a skill developed in one sport helps another sport more than the reverse.

How do we assess skill performance?

Initially, compare the visual feedback from the athlete's movement with the technical model to be achieved. Athletes should be encouraged to evaluate their own performance. In assessing the performance of an athlete, consider the following points: are the basics correct? Is the direction of the movement correct? Is the rhythm correct? It is vital to ask athletes to remember how it felt when correct examples of movement were demonstrated (kinaesthetic feedback). Appropriate checklists/notes can be used to assist the coach in the assessment of an athlete's technique.

How are faults caused?

After assessing the performance and identifying a fault, you need to determine why it is happening. Faults can be caused by an incorrect understanding of the movement by the athlete, poor physical abilities, poor coordination of movement, incorrect application of power, lack of concentration, inappropriate clothing or footwear, or external factors, e.g., weather conditions.

Strategies and Tactics

Strategies are the plans we prepare in advance of a competition that we hope will place an individual or team in a winning position. Tactics are how we put these strategies into action. Athletes in the associative phase of learning will not be able to cope with strategies, but those in the autonomous phase should be able to apply strategies and tactics. To develop strategies and tactics, we need to know the strengths and weaknesses of the opposition, our own strengths and weaknesses, and environmental factors.

"Practice makes permanent, but not necessarily perfect."

Mental Performance

Mental performance is just as important as physical performance in sports. A sports performance coach should work with athletes to develop mental skills such as focus, confidence, and resilience. Mental performance training can help athletes perform at their best under pressure.

Individuality

Every athlete is unique, and their training program should reflect that. As a sports performance coach, you need to take into consideration an athlete's strengths, weaknesses, goals, and injury history when designing their training program. A "one size fits all" approach will not work in sports performance coaching. So, you must do a AAA assessment.

Periodization

Periodization is the process of dividing an athlete's training program into different phases, each with a specific goal. This allows for optimal performance during competition season and reduces the risk of injury. A well-designed periodized program should include a preparation phase, competition phase, and recovery phase.

Progressive Overload

Progressive overload is the gradual increase of stress placed on an athlete's body during training. This stress can come in the form of increased weight, intensity, or volume. Progressive overload is essential for improving an athlete's performance and preventing injury.

Recovery and Regeneration

Recovery and regeneration are essential components of a sports performance program. Athletes need time to recover from the stresses placed on their bodies during training and competition. Recovery strategies such as massage, stretching, and foam rolling can help athletes recover faster and reduce the risk of injury.

Nutrition

Proper nutrition is critical for optimal sports performance. A sports performance coach should work with athletes to develop a nutrition plan that supports their training goals and lifestyle. The right balance of macronutrients (carbohydrates, protein, and fat) and micronutrients (vitamins and minerals) can help athletes perform at their best and recover faster.

Techniques for Improving Athletic Performance

Athletic performance is essential for every athlete who wants to achieve their goals and push their limits. Whether you are a football player, basketball player, soccer player, or any other athlete, you need to invest time and effort in improving your skills, strength, endurance, and mental toughness. In this chapter, we will discuss some of the most effective techniques for improving athletic performance that you can implement in your training and coaching programs.

Strength Training

Strength training is a fundamental component of any athletic performance program. It helps athletes build muscle mass, improve their strength, power, and explosiveness, and prevent injuries. As a coach or movement specialist, you should design a strength training program that targets the specific needs of your athletes and their sport. For example, football players require more upper-body strength, while basketball players need more lower-body strength.

Endurance Training

Endurance training is vital for athletes who participate in sports that require sustained physical effort over long periods. Endurance training can be achieved through activities such as long-distance running, cycling, and swimming. It helps athletes build their cardiovascular fitness, improve their endurance, and delay fatigue.

Mental Performance

Mental performance is an essential aspect of athletic performance that is often overlooked. It involves training the mind to handle the pressure, stay focused, and maintain a positive attitude. As a coach or movement specialist, you should incorporate mental performance techniques such as visualization, goal-setting, and mindfulness into your training programs to help your athletes stay mentally strong.

Nutrition

Nutrition is a crucial component of athletic performance. Athletes need to consume the right nutrients to fuel their bodies, repair muscles, and prevent injuries. As a coach or nutrition specialist, you should design a nutrition plan that meets the specific needs of your athletes, their sport, and their training regimen.

Injury Prevention and Rehabilitation:

Injuries are a common occurrence in sports, and they can significantly affect an athlete's performance. As a coach or movement specialist, you should incorporate injury prevention and rehabilitation techniques into your training programs to help your athletes stay healthy and recover from injuries quickly.

Speed and Agility Training:

Speed and agility training are essential for athletes who participate in sports that require quick movements, such as football, basketball, and soccer. As a coach or movement specialist, you should design a training program that targets the specific needs of your athletes and their sport.

Youth Sports Performance Coaching:

Youth sports performance coaching is essential for young athletes who want to develop their skills and improve their performance. As a coach, you should design training programs that are age-appropriate and focus on developing fundamental skills such as coordination, balance, and flexibility.

Post-Collegiate Sports Performance Coaching:

Post-collegiate sports performance coaching is essential for professional athletes who want to continue competing at the highest level. As a coach or movement specialist, you should design training programs that focus on maintaining the athlete's skills, strength, endurance, and mental toughness.

Recovery and Regeneration Coaching:

Recovery and regeneration coaching are essential for athletes who want to prevent injuries, improve their performance, and recover from intense training sessions. As a coach or movement specialist, you should incorporate recovery techniques such as stretching, massage, and foam rolling into your training programs to help your athletes recover quickly and perform at their best.

Conclusion

Improving athletic performance requires a comprehensive approach that targets various aspects of an athlete's training and lifestyle. As a coach or movement specialist, you should design training programs that are tailored to your athletes' needs and goals and incorporate the latest techniques and technologies to help them achieve their full potential.

Chapter 5: Assessing Athletic Performance

In the world of sports, assessing athletic performance is a crucial aspect that can make a significant difference in an athlete's career. As a coach or movement specialist, your role in assessing an athlete's performance can help them unlock their full potential and achieve their goals.

Assessing athletic performance involves a combination of physical, mental, and nutritional evaluations. It is essential to have a comprehensive understanding of the athlete's strengths, weaknesses, and areas for improvement to design a personalized training plan that can help them enhance their performance. Physical assessments are a critical component of evaluating an athlete's performance. These assessments help identify the athlete's physical abilities, such as strength, flexibility, speed, agility, and endurance. Strength and conditioning coaching for athletes can help them increase their strength and endurance, which can significantly impact their performance in sports.

Athlete Ability Assessment (AAA)

Over the years, I have assessed many players, and several have made it to the next level. One of the first players I had to evaluate was a young man named

Toledo Walls out of Pasadena City College. He came to me and said, "Coach, I need to get better." I assessed him and told him it wasn't going to happen in practice. We had to put in some extra work. This young man went on to play for Florida State and earn a national championship ring.

Over the years, I've known that assessing players is important to players. I had to evaluate Jaya Figueras; he was a young man from Glendale High School who played with a player I was recruiting. He came up to the school one day. He wasn't being recruited by many people. I said, "Well, let me see you work out." We made some adjustments and went and put a little work in. He went to an All-Star game, ended up becoming the Most Valuable Player, and then earned a scholarship to the University of Oregon.

I could go on and on, but I'm going to talk about the last player, Freddie Brown, a young man from Damien High School. I was training some other young men up at Chaffey College. One day, he came up and said somebody told him to come over and talk to me. I said, "OK, put your shoes on. Let me see what you got." To make a long story short, the young man ends up getting a scholarship to Utah and becomes one of the best receivers in the history of Utah football. Coaches start with a strong foundation of assessing an athlete with detailed precision to avoid costly roster mistakes in the end. You need to analyze your athletes to determine their strengths and weaknesses. The first step is to identify ideal attributes (e.g., biomechanical flaws, lower leg strength, and overall leg strength, athleticism (hips), multi-directional movement, speed acceleration, etc.). Doing this first will allow your coaches to achieve their agreed-upon goals.

Gap Analysis

The next step is to assess your athlete against your ideal athlete to identify their strengths and weaknesses. Addressing the gaps may require you to think about daily PSW planning, but for this macrocycle, you can set realistic drills with challenging goals to start addressing the gaps.

How do we assess skill performance?

Initially, compare the visual feedback from the athlete's movement with the technical model to be achieved. Athletes should be encouraged to evaluate their own performance. In assessing the performance of an athlete, consider the following points: Are the basics correct? Is the direction of the movement correct? Is the rhythm right?

It is important to ask athletes to remember how they felt when correct examples of the movement were demonstrated (kinesthetic feedback). Appropriate checklists/notes can be used to assist the coach in the assessment of an athlete's technique.

The following are some examples: lower leg strength, hip flexor, hip action, running technique, stop/decelerate footwork, reaction to sound, analytical testing starting speed, acceleration speed, change of direction speed, broad jump, and vertical leap.

What About Faults?

Having assessed the performance and identified that there is a fault, you then need to determine why that fault is happening.

Faults can be caused by an incorrect understanding of the movement by the athlete, poor physical abilities, poor coordination of movement, Incorrect application of Angle and force, lack of concentration, inappropriate clothing or footwear, and external factors, e.g., weather conditions.

Assessing an athlete's mental performance is equally important as evaluating their overall performance. Mental performance coaching for competitive sports can help athletes develop concentration, focus, and mental toughness, enabling them to perform at their best under pressure. Nutrition is another critical aspect that plays a crucial role in athletic performance. Nutrition coaching for athletes can help athletes understand the importance of proper nutrition and how it can impact their performance. Proper nutrition can significantly improve an athlete's endurance, recovery time, and overall well-being. Injury prevention and rehabilitation coaching for athletes are vital to ensure that athletes stay healthy and perform at their best. It is essential to identify potential injury risks and design a training plan that can reduce the risk of injury. Additionally, recovery and regeneration coaching can help athletes recover faster and reduce the risk of injuries. Youth sports performance coaching for young athletes can help young athletes develop proper techniques, prevent injuries, and enhance their overall performance. Post-collegiate sports performance coaching for professional athletes can help athletes transition from college sports to professional sports and develop new skills to perform at a higher level.

Developing Individualized Training Plans

One size does not fit all, especially when it comes to training plans for athletes. Every athlete has unique strengths, weaknesses, and goals, which means that their training plan should be tailored to their individual needs. Developing an individualized training plan can be a challenging task, but it is crucial for the success of an athlete. Here are some tips for coaches and movement specialists when creating a training plan for their athletes.

Assess Athlete Ability (AAA)

Before creating a training plan, coaches and movement specialists should assess the athlete's physical abilities, mental state, and goals. This will help them identify the athlete's strengths and weaknesses and create a plan that addresses both. The assessment can include physical tests, mental health evaluations, and interviews with the athlete to understand their goals, expectations, and motivation.

Set Realistic Goals

Setting realistic goals is essential for an athlete's success. Coaches and movement specialists should work with the athlete to set achievable short-term and long-term goals. Goals should be specific, measurable, achievable, relevant, and time-bound. Once goals are set, coaches can create a training plan that aligns with the athlete's objectives.

Create a Periodized Training Plan

A periodized training plan is a structured approach that breaks down an athlete's training into specific phases. The phases include the off-season, preseason, in-season, and post-season. Each phase has a specific focus and intensity level, and the training plan is adjusted accordingly. This approach helps athletes avoid burnout, stay motivated, and improve their performance.

Incorporate Variety

Athletes can quickly get bored with repetitive training routines. To keep them engaged and motivated, coaches should incorporate variety into their training plans. This can include different exercises, training methods, and environments. Variety can also help prevent injuries and improve overall fitness levels.

Monitor Progress

Monitoring an athlete's progress is essential for adjusting and modifying their training plan. Coaches and movement specialists should regularly assess the athlete's physical and mental state and track their progress toward their goals. This can include measuring strength, speed, endurance, and mental health. Adjustments can then be made to the training plan to address any weaknesses or areas for improvement. In conclusion, developing an individualized training plan is crucial for the success of an athlete. Coaches and movement specialists should assess the athlete, set realistic goals, create a periodized training plan, incorporate variety, and monitor progress. By following these tips, coaches can help athletes reach their full potential.

Conclusion

Assessing athletic performance is a critical aspect of sports-specific coaching for elite athletes. As a coach or movement specialist, it is essential to have a comprehensive understanding of the athlete's physical, mental, and nutritional capabilities to design a personalized training plan that can help them reach their full potential.

Chapter 6: Strength and Conditioning Coaching for Athletes

Fundamentals of Strength and Conditioning

Strength and conditioning are fundamental aspects of athletic performance that every coach should understand. Both aspects play a critical role in improving an athlete's ability to perform at an elite level, reducing injury risk, and enhancing overall health and longevity. In this chapter, we will explore the basics of strength and conditioning, including the principles of training, periodization, and the importance of recovery.

Strength training is the foundation of any athlete's physical development. It involves the use of resistance, such as weights, bands, or bodyweight, to create an adaptive response in the body. This response leads to an increase in muscular strength, power, and endurance. It is important to note that strength training should be specific to the athlete's sport and position to maximize performance gains. Conditioning, on the other hand, refers to the development of the cardiovascular and respiratory systems. It involves activities that increase the heart rate and breathing rate, such as running, cycling, or swimming. A well-designed conditioning program can improve an athlete's endurance and help them sustain high-intensity efforts for longer periods. The principles of training are essential to developing effective strength and conditioning programs. These include specificity, overload, progression, and individuality. Specificity refers to the idea that training should be tailored to the athlete's sport and position. Overload means that the athlete must be challenged with a workload that exceeds their current capabilities to see improvements. Progression involves gradually increasing the training load to avoid plateauing. Finally, individuality recognizes that each athlete has unique needs and responds differently to training.

Periodization is the organization of training into cycles or phases to optimize performance and reduce the risk of injury. These cycles may include a preparatory phase, a competition phase, and a transition phase.

The preparatory phase focuses on building a base level of strength and conditioning.

The competition phase involves finetuning the athlete's physical abilities to perform at their best during competition.

The transition phase allows for recovery and regeneration before the next training cycle.

Recovery is essential for athletes to perform at their best and avoid injury. Recovery strategies may include nutrition, hydration, sleep, stress management, and physical therapy. Proper recovery allows athletes to train harder and more frequently, leading to improved performance and longevity in their sport. In conclusion, understanding the fundamentals of strength and conditioning is critical to becoming an effective coach. By implementing these principles and strategies, coaches can help their athletes reach their full potential, reduce injury risk, and improve overall health and well-being.

Periodization for Strength and Conditioning

Periodization in strength and conditioning is the systematic planning of training to optimize performance and prevent injury. It involves dividing the year into distinct phases, each with a specific training focus, intensity, and volume. The goal is to manipulate training variables such as sets, reps, load, and rest periods to elicit specific adaptations and avoid overtraining.

There are several types of periodization models, including linear, undulating, and block periodization. The linear model involves gradually increasing the intensity and volume of training over several weeks or months, with periodic reloads to allow for recovery.

The undulating model varies the intensity and volume of training within each week or microcycle, while the block model focuses on specific training blocks with varying intensities and volumes. Regardless of the model used, periodization should be tailored to the individual athlete's goals, needs, and sport-specific demands. For example, a football player may need more strength and power in the off-season, while a cyclist may require more endurance and lactate threshold training.

In addition to the training focus, periodization should also consider recovery and regeneration strategies, such as nutrition, sleep, and active recovery techniques. Adequate rest and recovery are crucial for preventing overtraining and injury as well as optimizing performance. Periodization should also be flexible and adaptable to changes in an athlete's schedule, goals, or performance. It may need to be adjusted during the season based on the athlete's fatigue, injury status, or competition schedule.

In conclusion, periodization is a critical component of strength and conditioning training for athletes. It allows for a systematic and tailored approach to training, with a focus on optimizing performance and preventing injury. Coaches and movement specialists should consider the athlete's goals, needs, and sport-specific demands, as well as recovery and regeneration strategies, when designing a periodized training program.

Exercise Selection and Program Design

Exercise selection and program design are critical components of effective sports-specific coaching. Whether coaching elite athletes in football, basketball, soccer, or any other sport, it is essential to design a program that targets the specific needs of the athlete and their sport. This requires an understanding of the physiological demands of the sport, the athlete's individual strengths and weaknesses, and their training history. When designing a program, it is important to consider the athlete's goals and the specific demands of their sport. For example, a basketball player may require a program that emphasizes explosive movements, while a long-distance runner may require a program that emphasizes endurance. A comprehensive program should include exercises that target strength, power, speed, agility, and endurance, as well as mobility and flexibility.

Exercise selection is also critical. It is important to choose exercises that are specific to the athlete's sport and target the specific muscle groups and movements required for that sport. For example, a football player may benefit from exercises that target the muscles used in tackling, while a basketball player may benefit from exercises that target the muscles used in jumping. When designing a program, it is also important to consider the athlete's training history and current level of fitness. It is important to start with exercises that the athlete can perform safely and effectively and gradually progress to more challenging exercises as their fitness level improves. In addition to exercise selection and program design, it is important to consider other factors that can impact athletic performance, such as nutrition, injury prevention, and recovery and regeneration. A comprehensive sports-specific coaching program should address all of these factors to help athletes achieve their full potential. Overall, exercise selection and program design are critical components of effective sports-specific coaching. By designing a program that targets the specific needs of the athlete and their sport, coaches can help athletes achieve their full potential and excel in their chosen sport.

Monitoring Progress and Adjusting Training

One of the most critical aspects of coaching elite athletes is ensuring that they are constantly improving and progressing toward their goals. To achieve this, coaches need to monitor progress and adjust training accordingly. We will explore the best practices for monitoring progress and adjusting training to help athletes achieve their full potential. Monitoring Progress Monitoring progress is an essential part of any training program. It allows coaches to track an athlete's development and identify areas that require improvement.

There are several ways to monitor progress, including:

1. Performance testing is a great way to measure an athlete's progress. It involves testing specific skills or physical attributes, such as speed, power, and agility. Coaches can use this information to identify areas that need improvement and adjust training accordingly.

2. Video analysis is an effective way to identify technical flaws in an athlete's performance. Coaches can use video analysis to help athletes improve their technique and prevent injury.

3. Training logs are an excellent way to track an athlete's progress over time. They can include information such as training volume, intensity, and frequency. Coaches can use this information to adjust training and ensure that athletes are making progress

Adjusting Training

Adjusting training is essential to ensure that athletes are constantly improving. Coaches need to be able to identify areas that require improvement and adjust training accordingly. Some of the ways to adjust training include:

1. Periodization: Periodization involves dividing the training program into specific phases. Each phase

has a specific goal, and the training is adjusted accordingly. This helps to ensure that athletes are making progress and not plateauing.

2. Varied Training: Varied training involves incorporating different exercises and training methods into the program. This helps to prevent boredom and ensures that athletes are constantly being challenged.

3. Individualization: Individualization involves tailoring the training program to the individual athlete. This takes into account their strengths, weaknesses, and goals. This approach ensures that athletes are getting the most out of their training program.

Conclusion

Monitoring progress and adjusting training are critical aspects of coaching elite athletes. Coaches need to be able to identify areas that require improvement and adjust training accordingly. By using performance testing, video analysis, and training logs, coaches can monitor progress effectively. Adjusting training through periodization, varied training, and individualization ensures that athletes are constantly improving and progressing toward their goals.

Chapter 7: Endurance Training Coaching for Runners

Developing Endurance and Stamina

Endurance and stamina are integral components of an athlete's performance. Endurance refers to the ability to sustain prolonged physical activity, while stamina is the ability to maintain peak physical performance for an extended period. Developing endurance and stamina is vital for athletes in various sports, including football, basketball, soccer, and more. To develop endurance and stamina, athletes need to focus on a comprehensive training program that encompasses various aspects, including aerobic and anaerobic conditioning, nutrition, mental performance, injury prevention, and recovery.

Aerobic conditioning involves developing the cardiovascular system, which is responsible for delivering oxygen to the muscles. Aerobic activities, such as running, cycling, and swimming, are excellent for building endurance. Athletes should gradually increase the duration and intensity of their aerobic training to improve their endurance levels.

Anaerobic conditioning involves high-intensity activities that improve the body's ability to produce energy without oxygen. Anaerobic activities, such as weightlifting, sprinting, and high-intensity interval training (HIIT), are beneficial for developing stamina. Athletes should incorporate anaerobic training into their workouts to improve their speed, power, and explosiveness.

Nutrition plays a significant role in developing endurance and stamina. Athletes should consume a balanced diet that consists of complex carbohydrates, lean protein, and healthy fats. Hydration is also essential for maintaining optimal physical performance.

Mental performance is critical for athletes to maintain their endurance and stamina levels. Athletes should practice mental techniques such as visualization, positive self-talk, and goal-setting to improve their mental toughness and focus during competitions.

Injury prevention and recovery are crucial for developing endurance and stamina. Athletes should incorporate injury prevention exercises, such as stretching and foam rolling, into their training programs. Recovery techniques, such as massage, ice baths, and rest, can also help athletes recover faster and prevent overtraining.

In summary, developing endurance and stamina requires a comprehensive training program that encompasses various aspects, including aerobic and anaerobic conditioning, nutrition, mental performance, injury prevention, and recovery. With consistent training and dedication, athletes can improve their endurance and stamina levels and perform at their best in their respective sports.

Training for Long-Distance Running and Cycling

Long-distance running and cycling are two of the most challenging sports in terms of endurance, stamina, and mental toughness. To excel in these disciplines, athletes require training that is specifically tailored to their needs. In this chapter, we will explore the essential elements of training for long-distance running and cycling, including endurance training, strength and conditioning, nutrition, and mental performance.

Endurance Training: Long-distance running and cycling require a high level of endurance, which can only be achieved through consistent training. The key to building endurance is to gradually increase the duration and intensity of your workouts over time. This can be achieved through a combination of long and slow-distance runs or rides, interval training, and tempo runs or rides. It is essential to incorporate these workouts into your training plan to improve your aerobic capacity, increase your lactate threshold, and boost your overall endurance.

Strength and Conditioning: Strength and conditioning are also crucial components of training for long-distance running and cycling. These sports require a lot of lower body strength, especially in the quadriceps, hamstrings, and glutes. It is important to include exercises that target these muscle groups, such as squats, lunges, and deadlifts, in your strength training routine. Additionally, core strength is essential for maintaining proper form and preventing injury during long-distance runs or rides.

Nutrition: Proper nutrition is essential for long-distance athletes to perform at their best. To fuel your body for endurance activities, you need to consume a balanced diet that includes complex carbohydrates, lean proteins, healthy fats, and plenty of hydration. It is also essential to consume enough calories to support your training and recovery needs. During long-distance events, it is important to consume both carbohydrates and electrolytes to maintain energy levels and prevent dehydration.

Mental Performance: Long-distance running and cycling require a high level of mental toughness. To perform at your best, you need to develop mental strategies that help you stay focused, motivated, and confident. Visualization, positive self-talk, and goal-setting are all effective techniques that can help you stay mentally strong during training and competition.

In conclusion, training for long-distance running and cycling requires a comprehensive approach that includes endurance training, strength and conditioning, nutrition, and mental performance. By incorporating these elements into your training plan, you can unlock your full potential and achieve your goals as an endurance athlete.

Nutrition and Hydration for Endurance Athletes

Nutrition and hydration are crucial aspects of endurance sports, such as running, cycling, and triathlons. Endurance athletes require a higher intake of carbohydrates, protein, and healthy fats to fuel their bodies during long training sessions and races. Proper hydration is also essential to maintain performance and prevent dehydration.

Carbohydrates are the primary source of energy for endurance athletes. Athletes should aim to consume complex carbohydrates such as whole grains, fruits, and vegetables, as they provide a sustained release of energy during exercise. Simple carbohydrates such as sugars should be consumed sparingly, as they can cause a spike in blood sugar levels and lead to a crash in energy levels.

Protein is necessary for muscle recovery and growth. Endurance athletes should aim to consume protein-rich foods such as lean meats, fish, eggs, and dairy products. It is recommended that athletes consume 1.2–1.6 grams of protein per kilogram of body weight per day to meet their needs.

Healthy fats are also a crucial component of an endurance athlete's diet. Sources of healthy fats include nuts, seeds, avocados, and fatty fish. These foods provide essential fatty acids that help with energy production and can help reduce inflammation.

Hydration is essential for endurance athletes to maintain performance and prevent dehydration. Athletes should aim to consume 16–20 ounces of water before exercise and then 6–8 ounces every 20 minutes during exercise. Sports drinks can also be useful during longer workouts or races, as they provide electrolytes and carbohydrates to fuel the body.

In addition to proper nutrition and hydration, endurance athletes should also be mindful of their recovery strategies. Adequate rest and sleep are crucial for muscle recovery and injury prevention. Recovery strategies such as foam rolling, massage, and stretching can also help prevent injuries and improve performance.

Overall, proper nutrition and hydration are essential components of endurance sports. Athletes should aim to consume a balanced diet that includes complex carbohydrates, protein, and healthy fats while also staying hydrated and implementing recovery strategies to prevent injury and improve performance.

Recovery and Regeneration for Endurance Athletes

Endurance athletes, such as runners and cyclists, subject their bodies to intense physical activity that places a significant strain on their muscles. Therefore, recovery and regeneration are crucial components of their training regimen. Adequate recovery ensures that athletes can perform at their best and avoid injury.

Recovery and regeneration for endurance athletes involve several techniques that help reduce muscle soreness, improve flexibility, and enhance overall performance. One of the most effective strategies is proper nutrition. After a workout, athletes need to replenish their bodies with the right nutrients to promote muscle repair and growth.

A diet rich in carbohydrates, protein, and healthy fats is essential for endurance athletes. Carbohydrates provide energy for the body, while protein helps repair and build muscle tissue. Healthy fats, such as those found in nuts and seeds, are necessary for maintaining good health and providing energy for the body. Another crucial aspect of recovery and regeneration is adequate rest. Sleep is essential for muscle recovery, and endurance athletes should aim to get seven to nine hours of sleep each night.

Additionally, rest days are essential for recovery. Athletes should plan their training schedules to include rest days to allow their bodies to fully recover. Stretching and foam rolling are also effective techniques for promoting recovery and regeneration. Stretching helps to improve flexibility, which reduces the risk of injury. Foam rolling is a form of self-massage that helps to reduce muscle soreness and improve circulation. Massage therapy is another popular technique for promoting recovery and regeneration. Massages help reduce muscle tension, improve circulation, and promote relaxation. Athletes can also benefit from other recovery techniques such as ice baths, compression garments, and hydrotherapy.

In conclusion, recovery and regeneration are essential components of the training regimen for endurance athletes. Adequate nutrition, rest, stretching, foam rolling, massage therapy, and other recovery techniques can help reduce muscle soreness, improve flexibility, and enhance overall performance.

Coaches and movement specialists should work with athletes to develop a comprehensive recovery plan that meets their individual needs and goals. By incorporating recovery and regeneration techniques into their training regimen, endurance athletes can perform at their best and avoid injury.

Chapter 8: Mental Performance Coaching for Competitive Sports Mindset and Mental Fortitude

Mindset and Mental Fortitude

As a coach, you have probably heard the saying that sports are 90% mental and 10% physical. While the exact percentages may be up for debate, there is no denying that mindset and mental toughness play a significant role in an athlete's success. In this chapter, we will discuss how to develop a winning mindset and mental fortitude in your athletes.

First and foremost, it is essential to understand that a winning mindset starts with a positive attitude. A positive attitude not only helps athletes perform better but also helps them handle setbacks and challenges more effectively. As a coach, it is crucial to encourage your athletes to focus on the positive aspects of their performance and work on improving their weaknesses.

Mental fortitude is a vital element of a winning mindset. Athletes with this strength can push through physical and emotional challenges, emerging even more resilient. Such resilience can be cultivated through various techniques, such as visualization, self-talk, and goal-setting. As a coach, it's crucial to assist your athletes in building this mental endurance by introducing them to these methods and encouraging consistent practice.

Another critical aspect of developing a winning mindset is promoting a growth mindset in your athletes. A growth mindset is the belief that one's abilities can be developed through hard work and dedication. Athletes with a growth mindset are more likely to take on challenges and view setbacks as opportunities for growth. As a coach, it is crucial to encourage your athletes to adopt a growth mindset and help them develop the skills and strategies they need to succeed.

Finally, it is essential to understand the role of mental performance coaching in developing a winning mindset. Mental performance coaches can work with athletes to help them develop the mental skills they need to perform at their best. These skills may include visualization, relaxation techniques, and goal-setting. As a coach, it is essential to work with mental performance coaches to ensure that your athletes are receiving the support they need to develop a winning mindset. In conclusion, developing a winning mindset and mental training is essential for athletes to achieve success in sports. By promoting a positive attitude, mental training, and a growth mindset and working with mental performance coaches, coaches can help their athletes unlock their potential and achieve their goals.

Goal Setting and Performance Planning

Goal setting and performance planning are essential components of successful sports performance coaching. The process enables coaches to establish clear objectives and develop strategies for achieving them. With the right mindset and planning, athletes can unlock their potential and achieve their desired outcomes.

Setting SMART Goals.

The first step in goal setting and performance planning is to establish SMART goals. SMART stands for Specific, Measurable, Achievable, Relevant, and Time-bound. Specific goals are clear and concise, while measurable goals are quantifiable and trackable. Achievable goals are realistic and within reach, while relevant goals are aligned with the athlete's overall objectives. Time-bound goals have a specific deadline for completion. For example, if an athlete wants to improve their speed, a SMART goal could be to decrease their 40-yard dash time by 0.2 seconds within six weeks. This goal is specific, measurable, achievable, relevant, and time-bound.

Developing Strategies

Once SMART goals are established, coaches can develop strategies to achieve them. Strategies should be tailored to the athlete's strengths, weaknesses, and individual needs. For example, if an athlete wants to improve their speed, a strategy could be to focus on improving their technique through drills and exercises.

Monitoring Progress

Regular monitoring of progress is crucial to ensure that athletes are on track to achieve their goals. Coaches can use a variety of tools, such as performance metrics, video analysis, and feedback from the athlete, to assess progress. Adjustments may need to be made to the strategies if progress is not being made.

Celebrating Success

Finally, celebrating success is essential to reinforce positive behavior and motivate athletes to continue striving toward their goals. Coaches can recognize and celebrate achievements, no matter how small, to help athletes feel validated and encouraged.

In conclusion, goal setting and performance planning are critical components of successful sports performance coaching. By establishing SMART goals, developing tailored strategies, monitoring progress, and celebrating success, athletes can unlock their potential and achieve their desired outcomes.

Visualization and Imagery

Visualization and imagery are powerful tools that

coaches can use to help their athletes unlock their full potential. These techniques involve using mental images to improve performance and achieve specific goals. Visualization is the process of creating a mental image of the desired outcome, while imagery is the use of all the senses to create a mental representation of an action or event. Both techniques have been shown to be effective in enhancing performance, reducing anxiety, and improving focus.

In sports performance coaching, visualization and imagery can be used to help athletes prepare for competition by mentally rehearsing their performance. This can help them feel more confident and relaxed when it comes time to compete. Visualization can also be used to help athletes recover from injuries by imagining the healing process and visualizing themselves returning to competition.

Strength and conditioning coaching for athletes can also benefit from visualization and imagery. Athletes can use these techniques to improve their technique and form, which can lead to better performance and fewer injuries. By using mental images of proper form and technique, athletes can improve their muscle memory and reduce the risk of injury.

Endurance training coaching for runners and cyclists can also benefit from visualization and imagery. By imagining themselves crossing the finish line or completing a difficult training session, athletes can build mental toughness and increase their motivation to train harder. Visualization can also be used to help athletes overcome mental barriers, such as fear of failure or anxiety about a race.

In mental performance coaching for competitive sports, visualization and imagery are essential tools for improving focus and reducing anxiety. By imagining themselves performing at their best, athletes can create a positive mindset that can help them achieve their goals. Visualization can also be used to help athletes overcome negative thoughts or distractions that can interfere with their performance.

Nutrition coaching for athletes can also benefit from visualization and imagery. Athletes can use these techniques to visualize themselves making healthy food choices and eating foods that will fuel their performance. By creating a mental image of healthy eating habits, athletes can build better habits and improve their overall health and performance. Injury prevention and rehabilitation coaching for athletes can also benefit from visualization and imagery. Athletes can use these techniques to imagine themselves recovering from an injury and returning to competition. By creating a mental image of the healing process and visualizing themselves returning to competition, athletes can stay motivated and focused on their recovery.

Speed and agility training coaching for athletes can also benefit from visualization and imagery. Athletes can use these techniques to imagine themselves moving with speed and agility, which can improve their technique and form. By using mental images of proper form and technique, athletes can improve their muscle memory and reduce the risk of injury.

Sports-specific coaching for football, basketball, soccer, and other sports can also benefit from visualization and imagery. Athletes can use these techniques to mentally rehearse specific plays or scenarios, which can improve their performance on the field or court. Visualization can also be used to help athletes overcome mental barriers, such as fear of failure or anxiety about a game.

Youth sports performance coaching for young athletes can also benefit from visualization and imagery. By teaching young athletes these techniques, coaches can help them develop mental toughness and improve their focus. Visualization can also be used to help young athletes overcome fear of failure or anxiety about competition.

Post-collegiate sports performance coaching for professional athletes can also benefit from visualization and imagery. Athletes can use these techniques to mentally rehearse their performance and stay focused on their goals. Visualization can also be used to help athletes overcome mental barriers, such as fear of failure or anxiety about a game.

Recovery and regeneration coaching for athletes can also benefit from visualization and imagery. Athletes can use these techniques to imagine themselves recovering from a workout or competition, which can improve their recovery time and reduce the risk of injury. Visualization can also be used to help athletes relax and reduce stress, which can improve their overall health and performance.

In conclusion, visualization and imagery are powerful tools that coaches can use to help their athletes unlock their full potential.

These techniques can be used in sports performance coaching, strength and conditioning coaching, endurance training coaching, mental performance coaching, nutrition coaching, injury prevention, and rehabilitation coaching, speed and agility training coaching, sports-specific coaching, youth sports performance coaching, post-collegiate sports performance coaching, and recovery and regeneration coaching.

By using these techniques, coaches can help their athletes improve their technique, reduce the risk of injury, and achieve their goals.

Coping with Pressure and Stress

As a coach or movement specialist, you are likely aware of the immense pressure and stress that come with competitive sports. Whether you are working with young athletes or professional athletes, stress and pressure are inevitable. It is important to understand how to cope with these challenges and help your athletes do the same.

One of the first steps in coping with pressure and stress is acknowledging and accepting that it is a normal part of the sports experience. It is important to communicate this to your athletes and help them understand that feeling stressed or under pressure is not a sign of weakness. Encourage them to talk about their feelings and offer support when needed.

Another important aspect of coping with pressure and stress is developing healthy coping mechanisms. Encourage your athletes to engage in activities that help them relax and unwind, such as meditation, yoga, or listening to music. Encourage them to take breaks and engage in self-care activities like getting enough sleep, eating well, and spending time with family and friends.

As a coach or movement specialist, you can also help your athletes build resilience and mental toughness. This can be achieved through mental performance coaching, where athletes learn how to control their thoughts and emotions in high-pressure situations. Help them develop a positive mindset and focus on their strengths rather than their weaknesses.

It is also important to provide your athletes with the tools they need to manage stress and pressure during competition. This may include breathing exercises, visualization techniques, or self-talk strategies. Encourage them to develop a routine or ritual that helps them feel calm and focused before competition.

Finally, it is important to create a supportive team culture that values mental and emotional well-being. Encourage open communication, provide resources for athletes who may be struggling, and lead by example in taking care of your own mental health.

By helping your athletes cope with pressure and stress, you can unlock their potential and help them achieve their goals on and off the field. Remember that it takes a team effort to create a supportive and healthy environment for athletes to thrive.

Nutrition Coaching for Athletes

Nutrition is an essential component for athletes looking to achieve optimal performance on the field, court, track, or any other athletic arena. Proper nutrition provides athletes with the necessary fuel to perform at their best and helps them recover quickly between training sessions and games. The importance of nutrition for athletic performance cannot be overstated, as it is a key factor in determining an athlete's success.

Athletes who eat a well-balanced diet that is rich in carbohydrates, protein, and healthy fats have more energy and endurance during training and competitions. Carbohydrates are the primary source of energy for athletes, and they should consume enough of them to fuel their muscles during intense exercise. Protein, on the other hand, is essential for building and repairing muscles, which is necessary for athletes who are looking to increase their strength and power. Healthy fats are also essential for athletes, as they help to support the immune system, regulate hormones, and provide energy during long-duration activities.

Athletes who neglect their nutrition are at risk of developing nutritional deficiencies, which can negatively affect their performance and overall health. They may experience fatigue, muscle weakness, decreased endurance, and an increased risk of injury. In addition, athletes who do not meet their energy and nutrient needs may find it difficult to maintain a healthy body weight, which can also impact their performance.

Nutrition coaching for athletes is crucial, as it helps athletes to understand how their diet affects their performance and how to make informed choices about food and supplements. A nutrition coach can help athletes to create a personalized nutrition plan that is tailored to their specific needs and goals. They can provide guidance on meal timing, portion sizes, and hydration, as well as recommend supplements that can help to support athletic performance.

In summary, nutrition is a critical component of athletic performance, and athletes must pay close attention to their diet to achieve their maximum potential. Sports-specific coaching for elite athletes should include nutrition coaching as part of their training program to ensure that athletes are properly fueled and ready to perform at their best.

Macronutrients and Micronutrients for Athletes

As a movement specialist, coach, or sports performance coach, you have probably heard the terms 'macronutrients' and 'micronutrients' before. But what exactly do these terms mean, and how do they relate to the performance of elite athletes?

For athletes, it's important to consume the right balance of macronutrients to support their training and competition. Depending on the sport and individual needs, athletes may require higher or lower amounts of each macronutrient. For example, endurance athletes may need more carbohydrates to fuel their long-distance efforts, while strength and power athletes may require more protein to support muscle growth and recovery.

Micronutrients, on the other hand, are the nutrients that your body needs in smaller quantities but are still essential for overall health and performance. These include vitamins, minerals, and antioxidants. Vitamins and minerals play important roles in everything from bone health to immune function, while antioxidants help protect against damage from free radicals produced during exercise.

Athletes need to make sure they get enough of these micronutrients in their diets to support their training and competition. This can be challenging, as some micronutrients are only found in certain foods or may be lost during processing or cooking. Additionally, some athletes may have higher requirements for certain micronutrients due to the demands of their sport or individual factors like genetics or injury history.

As a coach, it's important to work with athletes to create a nutrition plan that ensures they are getting the right balance of macronutrients and micronutrients. This may involve working with a registered dietitian to assess individual needs and create a customized plan. It may also involve education and support to help athletes make healthy food choices and stay on track with their nutrition goals.

By understanding the role of macronutrients and micronutrients in athletic performance, coaches can help athletes unlock their full potential and achieve their goals. Whether you specialize in strength and conditioning, endurance training, mental performance, or sports-specific coaching, nutrition is a critical component of success.

Meal Planning and Timing

As a coach, you know that nutrition is a critical component of an athlete's performance. Adequate nutrition helps athletes maintain their energy levels, build and repair muscles, and improve their overall health and well-being. However, it's not just about what athletes eat but also when they eat it. Meal planning and timing play a vital role in optimizing an athlete's performance.

Meal planning involves creating a structured plan that outlines what an athlete will eat and when they will eat it. A well-planned meal should include a balance of macronutrients, including carbohydrates, proteins, and fats. Carbohydrates provide energy for the body, while proteins help build and repair muscle tissue. Fats provide essential fatty acids that the body needs for various functions, including hormone production.

When it comes to meal timing, it's essential to consider the timing of pre- and postworkout meals. Pre-workout meals should be consumed 2-3 hours before exercise to allow for digestion. These meals should be rich in carbohydrates to provide energy for the workout. Post-workout meals should be consumed within 30 minutes to an hour after exercise to help replenish glycogen stores and repair muscle tissue. These meals should include carbohydrates and proteins.

Athletes must also consider their individual needs when planning their meals. For example, endurance athletes may require more carbohydrates than strength athletes. Additionally, athletes with food sensitivities or allergies need to plan their meals accordingly.

In addition to meal planning and timing, coaches need to educate athletes on proper hydration. Dehydration can lead to decreased performance, fatigue, and even injury. Athletes should aim to consume at least half of their body weight in ounces of water each day.

As a coach, it's essential to work with a registered dietitian or nutritionist to develop a comprehensive meal plan for your athletes. This plan should take into account their specific needs and training goals. Additionally, coaches should monitor their athletes' progress and adjust their meal plans accordingly.

In conclusion, meal planning and timing are essential components of an athlete's performance. A well-planned meal that includes a balance of macronutrients and proper hydration can help athletes optimize their performance and achieve their goals. As a coach, it's vital to work with a registered dietitian or nutritionist to develop a comprehensive meal plan that meets your athletes' needs.

Supplements for Athletic Performance

Supplements can be a valuable addition to an athlete's training regimen, but they should never be a substitute for a well-rounded diet and training program. Before taking any supplements, athletes should consult with a qualified healthcare professional to ensure that they are safe and appropriate for their individual needs.

Creatine is a popular supplement among athletes, particularly those participating in high-intensity, short-duration sports like football and weightlifting. Creatine is a natural substance found in muscle cells that helps to produce energy during high-intensity exercise. Supplementing with creatine can help increase muscle strength, power, and endurance, but it may also cause water retention and gastrointestinal upset in some individuals.

Beta-alanine is another supplement that is commonly used by athletes. Beta-alanine is an amino acid that helps buffer the buildup of lactic acid in the muscles during high-intensity exercise. Supplementing with beta-alanine can help delay muscle fatigue and improve performance, particularly in endurance sports like running and cycling. However, some individuals may experience tingling or itching sensations after taking beta-alanine.

Caffeine is a natural stimulant that can improve mental alertness and physical performance. It is commonly found in coffee, tea, and energy drinks, but it is also available in supplement form. Athletes who use caffeine before exercise may experience increased endurance, improved reaction time, and reduced perception of effort. However, caffeine can also cause nervousness, jitters, and gastrointestinal upset in some individuals.

Fish oil is a supplement that is often recommended for its anti-inflammatory properties. Omega-3 fatty acids found in fish oil can help reduce inflammation and improve joint health, which may be beneficial for athletes who are prone to injury. Additionally, some studies suggest that fish oil may also improve cognitive function and mood.

In conclusion, supplements can be a useful tool for athletes looking to improve their performance, but they should never be a substitute for proper training and nutrition. Athletes should always consult with a qualified healthcare professional before taking any supplements to ensure that they are safe and appropriate for their individual needs.

Chapter 9: Injury Prevention and Rehabilitation Coaching for Athletes

Common Injuries in Sports

Sports are a great way to stay fit and healthy, but they can also be a source of injury if not done correctly. As a coach or movement specialist, it's important to understand the common injuries that can occur in sports and how to prevent them.

One of the most common injuries in sports is the sprain. This is when the ligaments that connect bones and joints together are stretched or torn. Sprains can occur in any joint, but they are most common in the ankle, knee, and wrist. To prevent sprains, athletes should make sure they warm up properly before exercising and wear appropriate footwear that provides support and stability.

Another common injury in sports is the strain. This is when the muscles or tendons that connect muscles to bones are stretched or torn. Strains can occur in any muscle group, but they are most common in the hamstrings, quadriceps, and lower back. To prevent strains, athletes should make sure they stretch properly before exercising and gradually increase the intensity of their workouts.

Concussions are also a common injury in sports, especially in contact sports like football and soccer. A concussion occurs when the brain is shaken inside the skull, causing a temporary impairment of brain function. To prevent concussions, athletes should wear appropriate protective gear and follow the rules of the sport to avoid head-to-head collisions.

Overuse injuries are another common type of injury in sports. These occur when an athlete performs the same motion or activity repeatedly, causing damage to muscles, tendons, and bones. Overuse injuries can occur in any part of the body, but they are most common in the shoulders, elbows, and knees. To prevent overuse injuries, athletes should vary their workouts and rest between sessions to allow their bodies to recover.

In conclusion, as a coach or movement specialist, it's important to be aware of the common injuries that can occur in sports and how to prevent them. By taking the necessary precautions and educating athletes, we can help them stay healthy and injury-free, allowing them to reach their full potential in their respective sports.

Preventing Injuries Through Training and Conditioning

Injuries are an inevitable part of sports, but they can be prevented through proper training and conditioning. As a movement specialist or coach, it is your responsibility to ensure that your athletes are physically prepared to compete at their highest level without putting themselves at risk of injury. This subchapter will explore the ways in which you can help your athletes prevent injuries through training and conditioning.

Strength and Conditioning Training.

Strength and conditioning training are essential for athletes to build the necessary musculature to withstand the physical demands of their sport. However, it is important that athletes are not, as this can cause muscle fatigue and lead to injuries. As a coach, you should design a strength and conditioning program that is tailored to you. This program should include exercises that focus on building strength, endurance, and flexibility.

Endurance Training

Endurance training is another important aspect of preventing injuries. Athletes who have poor endurance are more likely to experience fatigue during competition, which can lead to injuries. As a coach, you should design an endurance training program that is specific to your athlete's sport and position. This program should include exercises that focus on building cardiovascular endurance, such as long-distance running or cycling.

Mental Performance Training

Mental performance training is also an important aspect of injury prevention. Athletes who are mentally prepared for competition are less likely to make mistakes that can lead to injuries. As a coach, you should help your athletes develop mental skills, such as visualization, goal-setting, and positive self-talk, to help them stay focused and confident during competition.

Nutrition

Good nutrition is essential for preventing injuries. Athletes who are not properly nourished are more likely to experience fatigue, which can lead to injuries. As a coach, you should educate your athletes on the importance of proper nutrition and provide them with guidance on what to eat before, during, and after the competition.

Injury Prevention and Rehabilitation

Injury prevention and rehabilitation should also be a part of your training program. As a coach, you should educate your athletes on how to prevent injuries, such as through proper warm-up and cool-down routines, and provide them with resources for injury rehabilitation, such as physical therapy or chiropractic care.

Speed and Agility Training

Speed and agility training is important for athletes to perform at their best, but it can also be a source of injury if not done properly. As a coach, you should design a speed and agility training program that is specific to your athlete's sport and position. This program should include exercises that focus on building speed, agility, and coordination while also minimizing the risk of injury.

Youth Sports Performance Coaching.

Youth sports performance coaching is also an important aspect of injury prevention. As a coach, you should educate both parents and young athletes on the importance of proper training and conditioning to prevent injuries. You should also design a training program that is appropriate for the age and skill level of your young athletes.

Post-Collegiate Sports Performance Coaching

Post-collegiate sports performance coaching is important for professional athletes who are looking to take their game to the next level. As a coach, you should design a training program that is specific to the needs of your professional athlete, taking into account their position, strengths, and weaknesses.

Recovery and Regeneration Coaching

Recovery and regeneration coaching is essential for athletes to stay healthy and prevent injuries. As a coach, you should educate your athletes on the importance of rest and recovery and provide them with resources for recovery, such as massage therapy or yoga.

Conclusion

Preventing injuries through training and conditioning is essential for athletes to perform at their best and avoid unnecessary risks. As a movement specialist or coach, it is your responsibility to design a training program that is specific to your athlete's needs and goals while also minimizing the risk of injury.

By incorporating strength and conditioning training, endurance training, mental performance training, good nutrition, injury prevention, technical training and rehabilitation, speed and agility training, youth sports performance coaching, post-collegiate sports performance coaching, and recovery and regeneration coaching, you can help your athletes reach their full potential without putting themselves at risk of injury.

Rehabilitation Techniques for Injured Athletes

Rehabilitation Techniques for Injured Athletes Injuries are an inevitable part of sports and can occur at any time. As a movement specialist or coach, it is essential to have a good understanding of rehabilitation techniques for injured athletes to help them get back to optimal performance. In this subchapter, we will discuss various rehabilitation techniques that can be used to help injured athletes get back on track.

1. **Injury Assessment:** Before starting any rehabilitation program, it is crucial to assess the extent of the injury. This involves a thorough physical examination, medical history review, and diagnostic imaging, such as X-rays or MRI scans. The injury assessment will guide the rehabilitation program and help determine the level of activity that the athlete can undertake.

2. **Rest and Recovery**: Rest is a crucial part of the rehabilitation process. Athletes must allow their bodies to heal naturally, which involves taking a break from training and competition. During this time, the athlete can engage in low-impact activities such as swimming or cycling to maintain fitness levels.

3. **Physical Therapy**: Physical therapy involves a series of exercises and stretches that are designed to strengthen the affected area and improve the range of

motion. Physical therapy can be done in a clinic or at home with the guidance of a physical therapist.

4. **Strength Training:** Strength training is an essential component of rehabilitation that involves resistance training to build muscle and improve joint stability. Strength training should be done with the guidance of a strength and conditioning coach to ensure that the athlete does not aggravate the injury.

5. **Nutrition:** Nutrition plays a vital role in the rehabilitation process. A balanced diet that includes sufficient protein, carbohydrates, and healthy fats is essential for muscle recovery and repair.

6. **Mental Health**: Injuries can take a toll on an athlete's mental health, and it is essential to address this aspect of rehabilitation. Mental performance coaching can help athletes cope with the stress and anxiety that come with an injury and improve their mindset.

7. **Return to Play:** Before an athlete can return to competition, they must undergo a series of tests to ensure that they are fit to play. This involves a gradual progression of activity levels to ensure that the athlete's body can handle the demands of competition.

In conclusion, rehabilitation techniques for injured athletes are essential for getting them back to optimal performance. As a movement specialist or coach, it is crucial to have a good understanding of these techniques to help your athletes recover from injuries and prevent future injuries.

Return to Play Protocols

Return to Play Protocols injuries are a part of sports, and it is essential for coaches and movement specialists to have a plan in place to ensure a safe return to play for athletes. Return to Play (RTP) protocols are a set of guidelines that outline the steps an athlete must follow to return to their sport after an injury.

The RTP protocols vary depending on the type of injury, and the athlete's age, level of competition, and overall health status. However, there are some general steps that every RTP protocol should include.

Step 1: Medical Clearance

Before an athlete can return to play, they must receive medical clearance from a qualified healthcare professional. The healthcare professional will evaluate the athlete's injury and conduct tests and assessments to determine if the athlete is ready to return to play.

Step 2: Rehab and Conditioning

After medical clearance, the athlete must undergo a rehabilitation and conditioning program to strengthen the injured area and surrounding muscles. The rehab and conditioning program should be designed by a qualified strength and conditioning coach or physical therapist.

Step 3: Sport-Specific Skills

Once the athlete has completed the rehab and conditioning program, they must work on sport-specific skills. This step involves gradually reintroducing the athlete to the sport's demands, starting with basic skills and gradually increasing the intensity and complexity of the drills.

Step 4: Return to Play

The final step is the athlete's return to play. The athlete should start with low-intensity activities and gradually increase the intensity and duration of their performance. The coach or movement specialist should monitor the athlete's progress and adjust the RTP protocol if necessary.

Conclusion

The RTP protocols are critical for ensuring a safe return to play for athletes. It is essential to have a plan in place that is tailored to the athlete's injury, age, and level of competition. The RTP protocols should be designed by qualified healthcare professionals, strength and conditioning coaches, and movement specialists. By following the RTP protocols, coaches and movement specialists can help athletes return to their sport safely and confidently.

Chapter 10: Building A Solid Foundation

How To Strengthen Your Ankles & Feet To Improve Performance & Prevent Injuries

Over my career, I've always had the motto of building a solid foundation. This means I was talking about the foundation of the body and how the lower legs, feet, and ankle area are the foundation of the upper torso area. I was training a young man one day, and he had been in the NFL for four years. I asked him when we were starting to warm up, to walk on his toes for about 10 yards, and as he began, his ankles began to wobble. I asked him whether he had an ankle problem last year. And I told him that he had poor ankle strength.

He said he'd been in the NFL for four years, and nobody had ever said that to him. This is a very critical component for players to reach their full potential in sports. Foot and ankle training is a topic that is relatively neglected and overlooked in the field of kinesiology. However, proper activation and function of these areas are vital for maximizing performance and strength and are also critical for tissue health and injury prevention. Besides proper posture and spinal alignment, foot, and ankle function may be the single most crucial factor in optimizing movement quality, biomechanics, and muscle function if we're talking about building strength from the ground up, starting with the feet, ankles, and toes.

Feet and ankles affect everything!

For most movements, neural signaling begins at the feet. The better the feet and ankles are functioning, the better the innervation all the way up the kinetic chain, including signaling to the upper extremities. When the feet and ankles are in a state of dysfunction, any movement that requires even a slight degree of foot and ankle support becomes impossible to perform correctly. The action may look right on all accounts, but intramuscular and intermuscular coordination and overall motor unit recruitment are significantly compromised. This is something I refer to as 'pseudo-arthrokinematic manipulation.' It may look right to the eyes, but neuromuscularly, it's wrong.

Unfortunately, most athletes, lifters, and general populations display foot and ankle dysfunction to varying degrees, with most of them exhibiting externally rotated feet, valgus ankle collapse, and toe crowding (lack of space between the toes). Most high-level athletes have incredibly poorly functioning feet and ankles, with many of them having feet and toes that resemble those of disabled and physically impaired/dysfunctional individuals. No matter how strong, powerful, mobile, agile, fast, or explosive an athlete is, correcting these foot and ankle deficiencies will only improve their pre-existing biomotor capabilities.

The Impact on the Lower Body:

Addressing foot and ankle deficiencies will do wonders not only for strength and power but will also do more for technique and movement mechanics than most forms of corrective exercise. In fact, performing heavy lifts, particularly for the lower body, without proper foot and ankle mechanics only reinforces movement dysfunction. Many injuries, tweaks, and areas of general tightness, particularly in the lower body and lower torso, are related to faulty ankle and foot mechanics. If you consistently have tightness or pain in your hips, knees, or lower back, then your feet and ankles need addressing. In fact, it becomes impossible to squat or perform any other lower body movement correctly with faulty foot and ankle mechanics because hip and foot activation are directly related (one greatly impacts the other).

With that said, training the feet and ankles properly will immediately impact hip function, mobility, stability, muscle function, and lifting technique. Most untrained athletes run with their toes pointed downward. While they may have fast leg turnover, just like throwing a ball without using the wrist, the angle is missing unless the foot is dorsiflexed (pointing up) and ready to fire off the ground. Dorsiflexion of the ankle simply means to raise the toes and, in essence, cock the foot before striking the ground. This action engages the ankle and the foot for different angle generations, which can mean additional stride length for the athlete. The Claw drill and many of the skipping drills teach athletes to dorsiflex their feet. The ankle joint complex comprises the lower leg and the foot. It forms the kinetic linkage, allowing the lower limb to interact with the ground, a key requirement for gait and other activities of daily living. Despite bearing high compressive and shear forces during gait, the ankle's bony and ligamentous structure enables it to function with a high degree of stability. Compared with other joints, such as the hip or knee, it appears far less susceptible to degenerative processes such as osteoarthritis unless associated with prior trauma.

This chapter will highlight key anatomical bony structures and soft tissues that form the ankle joint complex, how the joint functions during walking, and how pathology changes these movements.

How to test your ankle mobility?

How do you know if you have poor ankle mobility? There are three primary ways to find out:

1. Perform a basic air squat a few times and have someone watch you. A telltale sign of poor mobility is if your heels routinely come off the ground.

2. Stand straight with your feet together. Can you lift the ball of your foot off the ground without moving your body?

3. Kneel on the ground and assume a position similar to stretching your hip flexors with one knee on the floor. The lead foot you are testing should be lined up five inches from the wall. Start to lean in toward the wall from this position while keeping your heel on the ground for as long as possible. This position allows you to measure the tibia angle in relation to the environment and the distance of the knee cap from the wall when the heel starts to come up. If the kneecap can touch the wall from five inches away, you have good mobility in the ankle.

How does poor dorsiflexion affect your performance?

Depending on the level of inflexibility in the ankle, it may cause a complete inability to perform a movement or create a negative knock-on effect all the way up the posterior chain with the serious potential to cause an injury. As I mentioned, poor ankle mobility causes the tibia to be dragged into a more vertical position, the trunk to lean forward, and the loss of a neutral spine, as well as a host of other maladies. What are the practical implications of poor dorsiflexion of the ankle? Primarily, it severely decreases the ability to generate maximum force, thanks largely to the loss of a neutral spine, impairing the ability to transfer energy from the hips to the load. In particular, it will affect your front squat (and therefore clean) and overhead squat (and thus snatch). Furthermore, suppose you are performing lighter or unweighted variations of these movements. In that case, you are building negative technique habits and unsafe joint loading patterns that will leak efficiency, reduce your work capacity, and increase the risk of injury.

Coaching Point: The biomechanics of the ankle have to do with the bony anatomy involved in the motion of the foot and ankle. The complexity of the ankle anatomy has a substantial influence on the biomechanical performance of the joint. When it comes to your athletes, it's important to discuss the motions of the ankle joint complex, the joints at which it is proposed they occur, and the ligaments that are critical to the stability and function of the ankle joint.

Big-ticket Items in Teaching Acceleration Techniques Several acceleration techniques can be taught in a few training sessions that will increase the speed of many athletes. Techniques like Ankle Dorsiflexion, Pocket Chin Arm Swings, Acceleration Position, and the grand prize of speed training, the Valsalva Acceleration Technique.

Dorsiflexion: Most untrained athletes run with

their toes pointed downward. While they may have fast leg turnover, just like throwing a ball without using the wrist, the power is missing unless the foot is dorsiflexed (pointing up) and ready to fire off the ground. Dorsiflexion of the ankle simply means to raise the toes and, in essence, cock the foot before striking the ground. This action engages the ankle and the foot for additional power generation, which can mean extra stride length for the athlete. The toe-tapping drill and many of the skipping drills teach athletes to dorsiflex their feet.

Pocket-Chin Arm Swings: Without exception, teaching proper arm mechanics for maximizing running speed is the most difficult. Many athletes do not see themselves unless they are taped, and they frequently gauge what they are doing with their arms based on their perception of how their arms feel during sprinting. In most cases, arm swings are incorrect and need repositioning. Pocket-chin is a good way of teaching arm mechanics and increasing overall speed.

The Butt Bumpers drill is the best drill I have seen for teaching correct arm swing mechanics. Have your athletes sit on the ground with both legs straight in front (side-by-side) and arms locked at 90 degrees. In slow motion, have athletes swing one arm backward until the hand reaches the pocket and one arm forward until the hand reaches chin level (approximately twelve inches away from the chin). This is the pocket-chin-level position. Performing this drill in slow motion initially is a good idea until the coach sees that the athletes are getting the feel of the arm positions. Move to half speed, then to full speed, for three sets of 5 to 10 seconds. If performed correctly, it is easy to see why this drill is called butt bumpers.

In 1970, I was taught to run with arm swings pointed in a straight line forward. Now we know that this instruction slightly restricts the hips during running and thus makes the athlete run slower. The arm swings should be pointed slightly toward the center of the body to maximize the hips, increasing stride length. Too much side-to-side movement will over-rotate the hips and cause problems. If an athlete points the arms past the center of the body, this can make the feet push off the surface in a duck-footed style rather than push the athlete straight toward the target. When you see a problem with the feet, look to the arms first for correction, as there may be an easy fix here. Challenge them to perform pocket-chin drills with "locked 90-degree arms" at home, looking in the mirror, sideways, and frontways.

Chapter 11: How To Increase Your Quickness And Speed

In this chapter, I will talk about a new concept of preparing for a sports competition. What makes plays and schemes work are athletes who can perform at a high level of skill and execute the right skill set with speed to perform specific routes.

I've asked coaches why they were doing particular drills with their players. I've told them that the exercises they are conducting with their players will not get them closer to their goals, to which some growled back because coaches can become entrenched in their coaching styles and methods.

Coaches need to shift their focus from drills to developing speed because speed is always a difference-maker.

The game has changed; strength is still necessary, but speed is the name of the game! When I work with athletes on speed, I start with their first step, and then I work on quickness, focusing on the first three steps and their ability to be explosive with high knees. The ability to have multi-directional movement yields a highly efficient player.

Acceleration Techniques and Speed Development:

By understanding the science and biomechanics behind acceleration techniques, your athlete's performance will increase exponentially. Athletes remember specific numbers for a lifetime. Most will never forget their personal best 40-yard sprint. Why do athletes remember their personal best speed forever? Speed is probably highly correlated with performance in most sports, and speed has been shown to predict athletic performance in college football in the USA.

For years, there were opinions about which tests were most valuable because no one really knew which, if any, of the tests would actually predict success for college athletes. A new study now provides the answers, and one of those answers is speed!

Speed is the quickness of movement of a limb, whether it is the legs, feet, or arm, and the angle of efficiency. Speed is an integral part of every sport and can be expressed as any one of, or a combination of, the following:

- Maximum speed.
- Elastic strength.
- Acceleration speed.

The three factors that affect speed are:

- Stride length,
- Strike rate (foot speed),
- Intensity.

The speed action used to develop the coordination of muscle contractions will increase speed. Repetition methods are used with a high number of sets, a low number of repetitions per set, and an intensity greater than 100% ballistic. In recent years, a system of selecting athletes for college and professional sports teams has evolved into several major physical tests involving speed, agility, and strength given to athletes on the same day. These tests are called the "Combines" in the USA. Having a good day at the combines can produce on-the-spot scholarships from prominent universities, and it can mean literally millions of dollars in sign-on bonuses and salaries for athletes entering the professional ranks. With the results of this new study, future "Combines" may focus on two acceleration tests. In the USA, the 40-yard sprint is king for many sports, except baseball, which uses the 60-yard distance required to run bases."

Developing Speed

An effective warm-up must consist of a series of dynamic and static movements that start with low-impact, low-intensity exercises and progress naturally to high-intensity, full-speed exercises that simulate the intensity of the upcoming practice or competition. As you know, for your athletes to be ready to perform speed work or compete at high intensities, they must get warmed up properly.

We often find that there is some confusion as to what constitutes a proper warm-up. Think about it: How often does an athlete hold a stretch position as part of their sport during a practice or competition? That is right—not very often. So, if you are still using this method to get your athletes ready to compete, you are not getting the most out of their abilities. Instead, have your athletes perform dynamic exercises similar to the types of movements they will be going through during practice and competitions. Keep athletes moving and gradually increase the intensity of their activity. That way, you can get the blood flowing into the muscles through a natural progression.

Remember, a good warm-up should take at least 20 to 25 minutes to complete. When they are done warming up, they will be lightly sweating, fired up, and ready to compete! This will reduce the likelihood of injury by ensuring that they do not try to go too fast too soon. In addition, athletes will get the most out of their muscles because they follow a thought-out progression of movements that go from low-intensity jogging and skipping to high-intensity speed development drills and exercises. Another issue to note when doing any type of drill is making sure that your athletes perform the exercises correctly. You compete as you practice. If athletes are not performing the drills correctly, they will increase the likelihood of injury by adding unnecessary stress to joints, muscles, ligaments, and tendons. Exercises are designed to be done a certain way for a specific reason. You must do the drill correctly because it trains your CNS, which over time trains your subconscious mind, which is your skillset. If your athletes are not technically sound during the warm-up and training, they will not be technically sound in games and competitions when it counts. The warm-up is not a time for goofing off. It is the foundation of the day's activities and sets the tempo for all to follow. So, now that you know what types of activities must be done and how to approach them, let us take a look at an actual dynamic warm-up that top athletes and coaches use to get ready each day.

Valsalva Acceleration Technique:

This is how a slower athlete can beat a faster athlete to the ball, to the hoop, to the tackle, to the touchdown, and to the finish line if the slower athlete is trained to hit the acceleration position (body straight, forward lean from the ankles) with arms pumping pocket-to-chin level. These are the keys to success in sports performance. I've used this drill exclusively with players for the last 30 years of my coaching career, and it has always made me an excellent coach. Getting my players to be explosive and have breakaway speed is especially important in all sports. I started using this in the '90s at Glendale College. I had a young man who was a running back named Peyton Rucker. I use this terminology of a car to describe how it accelerates and how it has a passing gear.

What is mental training? Mental training is verbal communication with the players. When you are driving a car and you want to go faster, you shift to a lower gear and accelerate your wheels' speed. I gave him an illustration. This is how illustrations can effectively train the CNS.

Understanding what acceleration and explosiveness mean:

There are different techniques you can use, such as visual aids and verbal communication, that players can understand.

The Valsalva technique is especially important when recruiting players. If the player has this already, it makes it a lot easier for you to coach. This is something you should be looking for in recruiting because it is a natural player who understands how to use God's gift to accelerate to an explosive position and speed. *Valsalva* is the technical term for acceleration, and tactically using the Valsalva acceleration technique at precise points will allow you to maintain your rhythm and maintain speed. If you look up the Valsalva maneuver on the internet, you will find that it describes briefly holding the breath. When applied properly for a brief burst of 2.5 seconds, this technique can be the single greatest producer of an instantaneous explosion in force, speed, and strength known in science.

Like many techniques, this one is so powerful that it can cause harm, but it also delivers championship plays. We all use the body's natural ability to increase strength by unconsciously performing the Valsalva maneuver. My favorite analogy to explain this to athletes is to describe a situation where the athlete's mom hands the athlete a jar with a tight lid. Mom needs some extra strength to open the jar, so she calls on the athlete for help. On the first attempt, the lid is too tight for the athlete. On the second attempt, the athlete increases the intensity and pushes hard with maximal effort. If you think about what the body does naturally in this situation, you will understand this valuable technique. The athlete tightens the abs and holds the breath for 2 or 3 seconds as maximum effort is applied. This is the Valsalva maneuver. The body increases blood pressure by an additional 100 points very quickly with this natural action. Clearly, this is dangerous to older adults with the potential for strokes, and it can be dangerous to some young athletes. But this technique will assist an athlete in opening the jar, lifting more weight maximally, and beating a faster athlete to the ball, goal, or finish line. An athlete cannot perform a maximum lift while inhaling, nor can an athlete quickly accelerate with full force while inhaling. The body was designed for the Valsalva maneuver and needed to be trained on how and when to deploy the technique.

Valsalva Acceleration Strategy Holding the breath too long can cause harm by making an athlete actually pass out. One occurrence is reported in the literature where this technique was responsible for bursting a tiny blood vessel in an athlete's eye during heavy maximal lifting. It is easy to observe that the Valsalva maneuver is frequently used safely as a natural function of the body to increase strength, but it is only held for two to three seconds naturally. A 100-meter sprinter would have time to plan for four Valsalva acceleration techniques during the short ten-second event, or a master sprinter like me may get in five before the finish. The miler may place the Valsalva acceleration technique in the race strategy 100 meters before the finish line to power that extra kick. The 400-meter sprinter may want to deploy this technique during the four handoff zones during the single lap around the track. The baseball player may wish to deploy this acceleration skill twice during the seven-second trip to first base. The football player may strategically use the Valsalva technique to break on the ball for a surprise steal. The applications for this acceleration technique are endless.

Conclusion

We have all seen the superstar athlete interviewed on television after making a game-winning play.

"How did you make that great play?" the reporter usually asks.

"I knew that the game depended on it. I gave it everything I had, and I made the play," seems to be the frequent answer.

That is what we hear, but the athlete should have explained: "I wanted to make the play, so I made the extra effort to get into the acceleration position (with a straight body bent from the knees), pumped my arms pocket-to chin level, and I positioned my shoulders lower to the ground than my competitor to drive my body forward toward the target. I took the extra energy necessary to apply the Valsalva technique to temporarily raise my blood pressure by an extra 100 points so I could get there faster than my competitor."

Some athletes make great plays without knowing the science of acceleration, but what if all your athletes trained with these techniques throughout the season? Perhaps this technique explains why some teams that do not match the physical attributes of stronger teams still find ways to win a championship. Perhaps the inferior team can realize that they had to go deep inside, work hard, get into the acceleration position on every play, and use the Valsalva technique to beat the superior team. "Whoever wants the victory the most will win this game," is what we tell the team. Perhaps we should train athletes to use this natural technique designed to assist the body in getting into maximal effort so athletes will have the skills necessary to beat a faster athlete and not wait until the game-winning play to deploy it. I rest my case here. Know that, Speed is a skill, and skills can be improved.

Tips on how to use this technique

I will give you some tips that I've used for years in developing this drill. Have your players take a 5-yard running head start and accelerate to full speed for 10 to 20 yards. Have them do this regularly. It will start to become second nature, which means we're training the central nervous system to react and respond quickly, so this is vital to use if you're going to be a football coach.

Chapter 12: Speed and Agility Training Coaching for Athletes

Developing Speed and Agility

Speed and agility are critical components of almost every sport, from football and soccer to basketball and track and field. As a coach or movement specialist, you have the power to help your athletes develop these vital skills and unlock their full potential.

There are numerous strategies and techniques you can use to improve your athletes' speed and agility, but it's important to remember that every athlete is unique. What works for one athlete may not work for another, so it's essential to tailor your approach to the individual needs and abilities of each athlete.

One effective strategy for developing speed and agility is to incorporate drills and exercises that focus on quick, explosive movements. Sprinting drills, agility ladders, and plyometric exercises can all help improve an athlete's speed and quickness, as well as their ability to change directions quickly.

Another key element of speed and agility training is developing proper technique. Proper running form, footwork, and body positioning can all have a significant impact on an athlete's speed and agility. Coaches and movement specialists should focus on teaching proper technique through drills and exercises that emphasize correct form and body positioning.

In addition to physical training, mental preparation can also play a crucial role in developing speed and agility. Visualization techniques, such as imagining oneself moving quickly and fluidly through a course or field, can help athletes build confidence and improve their overall performance on game day.

Nutrition and recovery are also critical components of speed and agility training. Proper fueling before and after workouts, as well as adequate rest and recovery time, can help ensure that athletes are performing at their best and can avoid injury.

Finally, injury prevention and rehabilitation should also be a focus for coaches and movement specialists. Proper warm-up and cool-down routines, as well as exercises that help strengthen and protect vulnerable areas of the body, can help athletes avoid common injuries that can hinder speed and agility.

Overall, developing speed and agility requires a holistic approach that combines physical training, mental preparation, proper nutrition and recovery, injury prevention and rehabilitation, and customized coaching to meet the unique needs of each athlete. With dedication and hard work, athletes can unlock their full potential and achieve success on the field or court.

Plyometric and Speed Drills

Plyometric and speed drills are essential for athletes who want to improve their explosive power, speed, and agility. These drills can be incorporated into any training program and can be tailored to specific sports. In this chapter, we will explore various plyometric and speed drills that can help athletes unlock their potential and improve their performance.

Plyometric drills are exercises that involve explosive movements, such as jumping, hopping, and bounding. These drills are designed to improve an athlete's power and explosiveness. Here are some of the most effective plyometric drills:

1. Depth jumps: This drill involves jumping off a box or platform and immediately jumping as high as possible when landing on the ground. This drill improves lower body power and explosiveness.

2. Box jumps: This drill involves jumping onto a box or platform from a standing position. This drill improves lower body power and explosiveness.

3. Lateral jumps: This drill involves jumping laterally over a hurdle or cone. This drill improves lateral quickness and agility.

4. Single-leg bounds: This drill involves jumping as far as possible on one leg. This drill improves single-leg power and explosiveness.

Speed Drills

Speed drills are exercises that focus on improving an athlete's running speed and technique. These drills can be done with or without equipment, and they can be tailored to specific sports. Here are some of the most effective speed drills:

1. Sprinting: This drill involves running at maximum speed for a short distance. This drill improves running speed and technique.

2. Shuttle runs: This drill involves running back and forth between two cones or markers. This drill improves acceleration and deceleration.

3. Resistance sprints: This drill involves running with a resistance band or sled. This drill improves sprinting power and explosiveness.

4. High knees: This drill involves running in place while lifting the knees as high as possible. This drill improves running technique and speed.

In conclusion, plyometric and speed drills are essential for athletes who want to improve their explosive power, speed, and agility. These drills can be incorporated into any training program and can be tailored to specific sports. By including these drills in your training program, you can unlock your potential and improve your performance.

Technique and Form for Speed and Agility.

Speed and agility are essential components of most sports. They require a combination of physical attributes such as strength, power, coordination, and balance, as well as a mastery of technique and form. In this section, we will explore the key principles that underpin effective speed and agility training and provide practical tips for coaches and movement specialists.

Focus on Technique First

Technique is critical for speed and agility. Before athletes can improve their speed or agility, they need to have a solid foundation in movement mechanics. This includes proper running technique, body positioning, and footwork. Coaches should prioritize teaching athletes the correct technique and form before worrying about increasing speed or agility. Without proper technique, athletes are more likely to get injured or plateau in their progress.

Use Progressive Drills and Exercises.

Once athletes have a strong foundation in technique, coaches can start to introduce more advanced drills and exercises to improve speed and agility. These should be progressive, starting with basic movements and gradually increasing in difficulty as athletes improve. For example, coaches can use ladder drills, cone drills, and plyometric exercises to develop speed and agility. These drills should challenge athletes but not overwhelm them.

Incorporate Strength and Conditioning

Strength and conditioning are also critical for speed and agility. Stronger muscles can generate more power, which translates into faster movements and better agility. Coaches should include strength and conditioning exercises as part of their overall training program. This includes exercises such as squats, lunges, deadlifts, and plyometrics.

Train for Specific Sports

Speed and agility training should be tailored to the specific demands of each sport. For example, soccer players need to be able to change direction quickly and accelerate rapidly, while basketball players need to be able to jump high and move laterally. Coaches should design their training programs with these demands in mind, focusing on the specific movements and skills needed for each sport.

Emphasize Recovery and Regeneration.

Finally, coaches should emphasize recovery and regeneration as part of their speed and agility training. Athletes need time to rest and recover between training sessions to avoid overtraining and injury. Coaches can incorporate strategies such as foam rolling, stretching, and massage to help athletes recover more quickly and effectively.

In conclusion, speed and agility are essential components of most sports. Coaches and movement specialists can use the principles outlined above to design effective training programs for their athletes. By focusing on technique, using progressive drills and exercises, incorporating strength and conditioning, training for specific sports, and emphasizing recovery and regeneration, athletes can improve their speed and agility and unlock their full potential.

Improving Reaction Time and Quickness

In sports, reaction time and quickness can often be the difference between winning and losing. A split-second delay in reacting to a play or opponent can mean missing a shot, losing a ball, or even risking injury. Therefore, improving reaction time and quickness should be a key element of any sports performance coaching program.

One way to enhance reaction time and quickness is

through specific drills that challenge the athlete's ability to react quickly to stimulus. For example, agility ladders, cones, and hurdles can be used to simulate game situations and improve footwork, reaction time, and coordination. These drills should be performed at different speeds and intensities to challenge the athlete's abilities and improve their reaction time and quickness.

Another way to improve reaction time and quickness is through strength training. Stronger muscles mean faster reactions and better control over movements. Therefore, incorporating exercises that focus on explosive power and speed, such as plyometrics and Olympic lifts, can help athletes develop the strength needed to react quickly and move faster.

In addition to physical training, mental performance coaching can also play a significant role in improving reaction time and quickness. Athletes must be mentally prepared and focused to react quickly to a play or opponent. Therefore, mental performance coaching can help athletes develop strategies to stay focused and calm under pressure, which can improve reaction time and quickness. Nutrition coaching can also be essential in improving reaction time and quickness. Eating a well-balanced diet that includes the right nutrients and hydration can help athletes maintain optimal performance levels. Adequate hydration is especially important in preventing fatigue and ensuring that the body can respond quickly to stimuli.

Finally, recovery and regeneration coaching can help athletes recover quickly from injuries and prevent future injuries. Rest and recovery are essential for athletes to perform at their best and reduce the risk of injury. Therefore, athletes should incorporate active recovery techniques, such as foam rolling and stretching, into their training regimen to reduce muscle soreness and improve flexibility.

Conclusion

Improving reaction time and quickness is critical for athletes looking to perform at their best. By incorporating specific drills, strength training, mental performance coaching, nutrition coaching, and recovery and regeneration coaching, athletes can improve their reaction time and quickness, reduce the risk of injury, and unlock their full potential.

Chapter 13: Sports-Specific Coaching for Football, Basketball, Soccer, etc.

Position-Specific Training for Football, Basketball, Soccer, etc.

Position-specific training is an essential aspect of coaching elite athletes in football, basketball, soccer, and other sports. This type of training is designed to improve an athlete's performance in their specific position, whether it's a quarterback in football, a point guard in basketball, or a striker in soccer.

To effectively carry out position-specific training, coaches must first understand the unique demands of each position. For example, a quarterback in football needs to have excellent throwing accuracy, while a striker in soccer needs to have speed and agility to get past defenders.

Once coaches have identified (AAA) the specific skills required for each position, they can design training programs that focus on developing those skills. This can include drills that simulate game situations, such as passing and shooting drills, and exercises that improve strength, speed, and agility.

It's also important to incorporate mental performance coaching into position-specific training. Athletes need to be mentally prepared to perform at their best, especially in high-pressure situations. Coaches can work with athletes to develop mental toughness, focus, and confidence, which can help them perform better on the field.

In addition to training, nutrition is also a critical factor in maximizing an athlete's potential. Coaches should work with athletes to develop meal plans that provide the necessary nutrients to support their training and recovery.

Injury prevention and rehabilitation coaching are also essential components of position-specific training. Coaches must be proactive in identifying potential injury risks and developing strategies to prevent them. If an athlete does suffer an injury, coaches should work closely with medical professionals to develop a rehabilitation program that will help them recover as quickly and safely as possible.

Finally, post-training recovery and regeneration coaching can help athletes recover from intense training sessions and prevent burnout. Coaches can incorporate rest days, stretching, and massage into their training programs to help athletes recover and perform at their best.

In conclusion, position-specific training is a critical aspect of coaching elite athletes in football, basketball, soccer, and other sports. By focusing on developing the specific skills required for each position, incorporating mental performance coaching, nutrition, injury prevention, and rehabilitation coaching, and recovery and regeneration coaching, coaches can help athletes reach their full potential and achieve success on the field.

Game-Specific Drills and Techniques

As a coach, it's important to understand that each sport has its unique set of skills and techniques. To help your athletes reach their full potential, you need to develop game-specific drills and techniques that will help them improve their performance on the field.

In this chapter, we'll explore some of the best game-specific drills and techniques that you can incorporate into your training program.

Football

One of the most important skills that football players need to master is ball control. To improve this skill, you can use the 'N and T-Cone' drill. This drill involves setting up three cones in the shape of a N or T and having the player around the cones while keeping them under control. Another important skill to master is tackling. To improve tackling, you can use the 'Tackle technique' drill. This drill involves setting up a five-cone and having the player practice tackling position in various ways.

Basketball

One of the key skills that basketball players need to master is shooting. To improve this skill, you can use the '10 Spot Shooting' drill. This drill involves setting up 10 spots on the court and having the player shoot from each spot. Another important skill to master is ball handling. To improve ball handling, you can use the "Around the World" drill. This drill involves having the player dribble the ball around their body in a circular motion.

Soccer

One of the most important skills that soccer players need to master is passing. To improve this skill, you can use the "Triangle Passing" drill. This drill involves setting up three cones in a triangle and having the player pass the ball to each cone in a specific order. Another important skill to master is shooting. To improve shooting, you can use the "Shooting on Goal" drill. This drill involves having the player shoot the ball at the goal from different angles.

These are just a few examples of game-specific drills and techniques that you can incorporate into your training program. Remember, the key to success is to develop a training program that is tailored to the needs of your athletes. By doing so, you'll help them reach their full potential and achieve their goals on the field.

Developing Tactical Awareness and Game IQ

Tactical awareness and game IQ are crucial components of any athlete's success in their respective sport. These attributes enable an athlete to understand and anticipate the game's flow, make quick decisions, and execute effective strategies to outsmart their opponents. In this chapter, we will explore how coaches can help athletes develop their tactical awareness and game IQ.

Firstly, coaches must ensure that their athletes have a solid understanding of the game's rules and regulations. This knowledge can help athletes make better decisions, avoid penalties, and take advantage of opportunities that may arise during the game.

Secondly, coaches must teach their athletes to analyze and understand their opponents' strategies and tendencies. This knowledge can help athletes anticipate their opponents' moves and make quick decisions to counter their attacks effectively.

Thirdly, coaches must encourage their athletes to develop their situational awareness. Athletes must be able to read and react to various game situations, such as understanding when to make a play or when to hold back and defend.

Fourthly, coaches must teach their athletes to communicate effectively on the field. Clear communication can help prevent mistakes and misunderstandings, leading to better teamwork and overall performance.

Lastly, coaches must expose their athletes to different game scenarios and encourage them to think critically about how to handle each situation. This exposure can help athletes develop their game IQ and prepare them for unpredictable situations that may arise.

In conclusion, developing tactical awareness and game IQ is essential for athletes' success in their respective sports. Coaches must ensure that their athletes have a solid understanding of the game, opponents, situational awareness, communication, and exposure to different game scenarios. By doing so, coaches can help their athletes unlock their full potential and achieve their goals.

Maximizing Athletic Potential for Specific Sports

Athletes who are seeking to improve their performance in specific sports need to have a well-rounded training program that focuses on their strengths and weaknesses. Maximizing athletic potential requires more than just physical training; it also requires mental preparation, proper nutrition, and recovery techniques. In this chapter, we will explore how to maximize athletic potential for specific sports.

Sports Performance Coaching

Sports performance coaching is focused on helping athletes develop and enhance their performance in their respective sports. This type of coaching includes developing strength, speed, agility, and endurance. Sports performance coaching also involves mental preparation and visualization techniques to help athletes stay focused and motivated during competitions.

Strength and Speed Coaching for Athletes.

Strength and speed coaching is essential for athletes as it helps them develop the physical strength and endurance needed for their specific sport. This type of training includes weightlifting, resistance training, speed training, and cardiovascular training. The coach works closely with the athlete to develop an individualized program that focuses on their specific needs.

Endurance Training Coaching for Runners and Cyclists

Endurance training coaching is focused on developing the athlete's cardiovascular endurance, which is crucial for runners and cyclists. This type of training includes long-distance running, cycling, and interval training. The coach works closely with the athlete to develop a program that focuses on their specific needs and goals.

Mental Performance Coaching for Competitive Sports

Mental performance coaching is essential for athletes as it helps them develop the mental toughness needed to perform at their best during competitions. This type of coaching includes visualization techniques, goal setting, and stress management. The coach works closely with the athlete to develop a program that helps them stay focused and motivated during competitions.

Nutrition Coaching for Athletes.

Nutrition coaching is essential for athletes as it helps them develop a healthy and balanced diet that provides them with the necessary nutrients needed for their specific sport. The coach works closely with the athlete to develop a program that includes healthy eating habits, meal planning, and hydration.

Injury Prevention and Rehabilitation Coaching for Athletes

Injury prevention and rehabilitation coaching are focused on helping athletes prevent injuries and recover from injuries. The coach works closely with the athlete to develop a program that includes injury prevention techniques, stretching, and rehabilitation exercises.

Speed and Agility Training Coaching for Athletes

Speed and agility training coaching is essential for athletes as it helps them develop the speed and agility needed for their specific sport. This type of training includes sprinting, plyometrics, and agility drills. The coach works closely with the athlete to develop a program that focuses on their specific needs.

Sports-Specific Coaching for Football, Basketball, Soccer, etc.

Sports-specific coaching is focused on developing the skills needed for a specific sport, such as football, basketball, or soccer. This type of coaching includes developing skills such as ball control, passing, shooting, and defending. The coach works closely with the athlete to develop a program that focuses on their specific needs.

Youth Sports Performance Coaching for Young Athletes

Youth sports performance coaching is essential for young athletes as it helps them develop the physical and mental skills needed for their specific sport. This type of coaching includes developing skills such as coordination, balance, and endurance. The coach works closely with the athlete to develop a program that focuses on their specific needs and goals.

Post-Collegiate Sports Performance Coaching for Professional Athletes

Post-collegiate sports performance coaching is focused on helping professional athletes maintain their physical and mental skills as they age. This type of coaching includes developing skills such as strength, endurance, and mental toughness. The coach works closely with the athlete to develop a program that focuses on their specific needs and goals.

Recovery and Regeneration Coaching for Athletes.

Recovery and regeneration coaching is essential for athletes as it helps them recover from training and competitions. This type of coaching includes rest, massage, and stretching. The coach works closely with the athlete to develop a program that focuses on their specific needs.

In conclusion, maximizing athletic potential for specific sports requires a well-rounded training program that focuses on physical training, mental preparation, proper nutrition, and recovery techniques. By working with a coach who specializes in sports performance coaching, athletes can develop the skills and endurance needed to excel in their respective sports.

Youth Sports Performance Coaching for Young Athletes

Fundamentals of Youth Sports Performance Coaching

Youth sports performance coaching is a critical component of any athlete's development. Children and teenagers have unique physical, psychological, and social needs that require specialized coaching techniques to help them reach their full potential. In this subchapter, we will explore the fundamentals of youth sports performance coaching, including the importance of early specialization, long-term athlete development, and age-appropriate training methods.

Early specialization is a controversial topic in youth sports. Some argue that children should play multiple sports to develop a broad range of physical and cognitive skills. Others believe that early specialization in a particular sport is necessary for success at the highest levels. However, recent research suggests that early specialization is not the key to success. Instead, a well-rounded athletic background that includes exposure to multiple sports and activities can enhance an athlete's physical and mental abilities.

Long-term athlete development is another critical concept in youth sports performance coaching. The goal of long-term athlete development is to create a sustainable model of athlete development that takes into account the unique needs of young athletes. This includes understanding the stages of physical, cognitive, and emotional development and designing training programs that align with these stages. Coaches must also consider the social and environmental factors that influence an athlete's development, such as family support, access to resources, and cultural norms.

Age-appropriate training methods are essential for youth sports performance coaching. Children and teenagers have different physical and psychological needs than adults, and coaches must adjust their training methods accordingly. For example, younger athletes may require more emphasis on physical fundamentals, such as balance, coordination, and body awareness. As athletes progress in age, coaches should shift their focus to more advanced skills, such as speed, agility, and strength.

In conclusion, youth sports performance coaching

is a critical component of any athlete's development. Coaches must understand the unique needs of young athletes and design training programs that align with these needs. This includes early specialization, long-term athlete development, and age-appropriate training methods. By following these fundamentals, coaches can help young athletes reach their full potential and lay the foundation for success at the highest levels of competition.

Developmentally Appropriate Training Techniques

When it comes to coaching elite athletes, it's critical to understand the importance of developmentally appropriate training techniques. These techniques are designed to meet the unique needs of athletes at different stages of their development, from young children to professional athletes.

For sports performance coaching, it's essential to understand that young athletes have different physical and mental capacities than older athletes. Young athletes require a different approach to training that focuses on developing their coordination, balance, and foundational strength. As they progress, they can gradually increase their intensity and volume of training. Strength and conditioning coaching for athletes should focus on developing a foundation of strength, power, and endurance. This foundation should be built through exercises that are appropriate for the athlete's age, skill level, and sport. As athletes progress, their training should become more sport-specific, incorporating exercises that mimic the movements and demands of their sport.

Endurance training coaching for runners and cyclists should focus on developing cardiovascular fitness, muscular endurance, and lactate threshold. This type of training should be progressive and tailored to the athlete's current fitness level, with an emphasis on building endurance gradually over time.

Mental performance coaching for competitive sports should focus on developing mental skills such as focus, confidence, and resilience. These skills can be developed through visualization, goal-setting, and mindfulness practices.

Nutrition coaching for athletes is critical for optimal performance and recovery. Athletes should be educated on the importance of proper hydration, nutrient timing, and fueling strategies for their sport.

Injury prevention and rehabilitation coaching for athletes is essential for keeping athletes healthy and on the field. Coaches should focus on developing injury prevention programs that address the specific needs of their sport and athletes. In the event of an injury, coaches should work closely with athletic trainers and medical professionals to provide appropriate rehabilitation and return-to-play protocols.

Speed and agility training coaching for athletes should focus on developing quickness, agility, and reaction time. These skills can be developed through a variety of drills and exercises that are appropriate for the athlete's sport and skill level.

Sports-specific coaching for football, basketball, soccer, and other sports should focus on developing the specific skills and movements required for that sport. Coaches should use drills and exercises that mimic the demands of the sport and progressively increase the intensity and complexity of training.

Youth sports performance coaching for young athletes should be age-appropriate, focusing on developing foundational skills such as coordination, balance, and strength. As athletes progress, coaches can gradually increase the volume and intensity of training.

Recovery and regeneration coaching for athletes is critical for optimizing performance and preventing injury. Coaches should focus on developing recovery strategies such as active recovery, mobility work, and sleep hygiene to help athletes recover and perform at their best.

Overall, developmentally appropriate training techniques are critical for coaching elite athletes. Coaches should focus on tailoring their training programs to meet the unique needs of each athlete, taking into account their age, skill level, and sport-specific demands. By doing so, coaches can help athletes unlock their full potential and achieve their goals.

Age-Specific Training Plans

As a coach or movement specialist, it is essential to understand that athletes of different age groups have varying physical, emotional, and psychological capabilities. Therefore, designing training plans that cater to the unique needs of each age group is crucial in unlocking the potential of elite athletes.

Youth Sports Performance Coaching for Young Athletes

For young athletes aged between 6 and 12 years, the focus should be on developing motor skills, coordination, and balance through fun and engaging activities. At this age, children have a short attention span, and the training should be kept simple and engaging to maintain their interest. Training sessions should be kept short, between 30 to 45 minutes, and should include a lot of play-based activities.

Strength and Conditioning Coaching for Athletes

Strength and conditioning training is crucial for athletes aged between 13 and 18 years. At this age, the focus should be on building strength, endurance, and power. The training should be more structured and intense, with a focus on developing the right technique to prevent injuries. The training sessions should be between 60 and 90 minutes, and the program should be progressive to help the athlete reach their full potential.

Post-Collegiate Sports Performance Coaching for Professional Athletes

For professional athletes aged between 22 and 35 years, the focus should be on maintaining peak performance while preventing injuries. The training should be tailored to the athlete's specific needs, taking into consideration their sport, position, and individual strengths and weaknesses. The training should be more advanced and challenging, focusing on power, speed, agility, and endurance.

Recovery and Regeneration Coaching for Athletes

Recovery and regeneration are crucial for athletes of all ages. As athletes get older, their bodies take longer to recover from training and competition. Therefore, it is essential to include recovery sessions in the training plan. These sessions should include stretching, foam rolling, massage, and other recovery techniques to help the athlete's body recover faster.

In conclusion, designing age-specific training plans is crucial in unlocking the potential of elite athletes. As a coach or movement specialist, it is essential to understand the unique needs of each age group to design a training plan that caters to their specific needs. By doing so, you can help your athletes reach their full potential while keeping them injury-free.

Mental and Emotional Development of Young Athletes

The mental and emotional development of young athletes is critical to their success in sports. As a coach or movement specialist, understanding the psychological aspects of your young athletes is just as important as their physical development. In some cases, mental preparation can even make the difference between winning and losing.

One of the most important aspects to consider in the mental and emotional development of young athletes is their self-esteem. As a coach, it is important to create a positive environment that fosters confidence and self-belief. Acknowledging their accomplishments and offering constructive feedback can go a long way in building their confidence and self-esteem.

Another important aspect is managing their emotions. Sports can be an emotional roller coaster for young athletes, and it is important for coaches to help them manage their emotions in a healthy and productive way. Encouraging them to express their emotions and teaching them coping mechanisms can help them deal with the pressures of competition and the ups and downs of training.

Furthermore, mental toughness is another critical aspect of mental and emotional development in sports. Teaching young athletes to overcome setbacks and push through challenging times can help them develop the mental toughness they need to succeed. This can be achieved through visualization and positive self-talk, as well as through challenging training sessions that push their limits.

Finally, instilling a growth mindset in young athletes can also help them develop mentally and emotionally. This means teaching them to embrace challenges and see failure as an opportunity to learn and grow. By fostering a growth mindset, coaches can help their young athletes stay motivated and continue to improve over time.

In conclusion, the mental and emotional development of young athletes is crucial to their success in sports. As a coach or movement specialist, it is important to create a positive environment that fosters confidence and self-esteem, helps manage emotions, develops mental toughness, and instills a growth mindset. By focusing on these aspects, you can help your young athletes unlock their full potential and achieve success in their sports.

Chapter 14: Post-Collegiate Sports Performance Coaching for Professional Athletes

Transitioning from College to Professional Sports

Moving from college to professional sports is a significant transition for any athlete. The jump from college to the pros is not just a leap in competition but also a change in lifestyle. As a coach or movement specialist, you have a critical role in preparing your athletes for this transition. Here are some essential factors to consider when helping your athletes make the jump:

Competition Level

The competition level in professional sports is higher than in college sports. The athletes are more skilled, faster, and stronger. The game is more intense, and the pressure to perform is higher. As a coach, you need to prepare your athletes mentally and physically for this level of competition.

Fitness Level

Professional sports require a higher level of fitness than college sports. Athletes need to be in peak physical condition to compete at this level. As a coach, you need to ensure that your athletes are training at the right intensity and volume to reach their maximum physical potential.

Lifestyle

Professional sports come with a different lifestyle than college sports. Athletes need to manage their time, finances, and relationships differently. As a coach, you need to help your athletes prepare for this change and support them through the transition.

Mental Toughness

Professional sports require mental toughness to succeed. Athletes need to be able to handle pressure, deal with setbacks, and manage their emotions. As a coach, you need to help your athletes develop mental toughness through mental performance coaching and other strategies.

Nutrition

Nutrition is critical for professional athletes. Athletes need to fuel their bodies with the right nutrients to perform at their best. As a coach, you need to work with your athletes to develop a nutrition plan that will support their training and competition.

Injury Prevention and Rehabilitation

Injuries are a part of sports, but they can also be prevented. As a coach, you need to help your athletes develop proper injury prevention strategies and rehabilitation plans to ensure they stay healthy and on the field.

Recovery and Regeneration

Professional athletes need to prioritize recovery and regeneration. Adequate sleep, nutrition, and active recovery are essential for optimal performance. As a coach, you can help your athletes develop a recovery and regeneration plan that will support their training and competition.

In conclusion, the transition from college to professional sports requires preparation and support from coaches and movement specialists. By considering these essential factors, you can help your athletes make a successful transition and reach their full potential in their professional careers.

Specialized Training and Conditioning for Professional Athletes

Specialized Training and Conditioning for Professional Athletes

Professional Athletes are a unique breed of individuals who require specialized training and conditioning techniques to reach their full potential.

These athletes are at the pinnacle of their sport and must maintain their physical and mental abilities to continue performing at the highest level. To achieve this, coaches and movement specialists must understand the specific needs of each athlete and tailor their training and conditioning program accordingly.

Strength and Conditioning Coaching for Athletes

Strength and conditioning coaching is an essential component of any professional athlete's training program. It involves developing strength, power, speed, agility, and endurance to improve overall performance. This training is typically tailored to the specific needs of individual athletes, taking into account their sport, position, and physical condition.

Endurance Training Coaching for Runners and Cyclists.

Endurance training is vital for runners and cyclists, as it improves their cardiovascular fitness and allows them to perform at a high level for extended periods. Coaches must implement training programs that focus on building endurance, increasing VO2 max, and improving lactate threshold.

Mental Performance Coaching for Competitive Sports

Mental performance coaching is becoming

increasingly popular in professional sports. It involves developing mental skills such as focus, concentration, visualization, and self-confidence. Coaches must work closely with athletes to help them develop these skills and overcome mental barriers that may be holding them back.

Nutrition Coaching for Athletes

Nutrition is a critical component of any athlete's training program. Coaches must work with their athletes to develop a nutrition plan that will support their training, recovery, and overall health. This plan should include the right balance of macronutrients, micronutrients, and hydration.

Injury Prevention and Rehabilitation Coaching for Athletes.

Injuries are a common occurrence in professional sports, and coaches must work to prevent them and help athletes recover quickly. Injury prevention strategies may include strengthening exercises, flexibility training, and proper technique. Rehabilitation programs must be tailored to the specific injury and the athlete's needs.

Speed and Agility Training Coaching for Athletes

Speed and agility are critical components of many sports, and coaches must develop training programs that focus on these skills. This training may include plyometrics, sprinting drills, and agility exercises.

Sports-Specific Coaching for Football, Basketball, Soccer, etc.

Each sport requires a unique set of skills, and coaches must develop training programs that focus on these skills. Sports-specific coaching may include position-specific training, tactical drills, and game simulations.

Post-Collegiate Sports Performance Coaching for Professional Athletes

Professional athletes require specialized training programs that focus on maintaining their physical and mental abilities. Coaches must work to develop programs that support recovery, regeneration, and injury prevention.

Recovery and Regeneration Coaching for Athletes

Recovery and regeneration are critical components of any professional athlete's training program. Coaches must develop strategies that support recovery, such as sleep, nutrition, and hydration. Regeneration may include massage, stretching, and foam rolling.

In conclusion, specialized training and speed are essential for professional athletes to maintain their physical and mental abilities. Coaches and movement specialists must understand the specific needs of each athlete and tailor their programs accordingly. These programs may include speed performance training technical coaching, strength and conditioning coaching, endurance training coaching, mental performance coaching, nutrition coaching, injury prevention, and rehabilitation coaching, speed and agility training coaching, sports-specific coaching, youth sports performance coaching, post-collegiate sports performance coaching, and recovery and regeneration coaching. With a specialized training program in place, professional athletes can unlock their full potential and achieve success in their sport.

Injury Prevention and Rehabilitation for Professional Athletes

Professional athletes are no strangers to injuries. In fact, injuries are almost inevitable in any sport. However, the key to a successful career in sports is not just about being able to perform at a high level but also being able to minimize and recover from injuries effectively. Here, we will discuss injury prevention and rehabilitation strategies that will help professional athletes stay healthy and perform at their best.

Prevention Strategies

Preventing injuries should be a top priority for

professional athletes. Here are a few strategies that can help:

1. A good warm-up routine can help prepare the body for the physical demands of the sport and reduce the risk of injury. Proper Warm-Up

2. Strength Training: Strength training can help improve muscle strength and endurance, which can reduce the risk of injury.

3. Proper technique is critical in preventing injuries. Coaches and trainers should focus on teaching athletes proper form and technique for their sport.

4. Recovery Time: Adequate rest and recovery time are essential for preventing injuries. Athletes should be given enough time to recover after games and practices.

Rehabilitation Strategies

Injuries are a part of sports, and when they do occur, it is important to have a rehabilitation plan in place. Here are a few strategies that can help:

1. Rest and Recovery: Rest and recovery are critical for healing from injuries. Athletes should be given enough time to rest and recover before returning to their sport.

2. Physical Therapy: Physical therapy can help athletes recover from injuries by improving their range of motion, flexibility, and strength.

3. Proper Nutrition: Proper nutrition is essential for the body to heal and recover from injuries. Athletes should focus on eating a balanced diet that includes plenty of protein, carbohydrates, and healthy fats.

4. Mental Health: Injuries can take a toll on an athlete's mental health. Coaches and trainers should provide support and resources to help athletes cope with the mental and emotional effects of injuries.

In conclusion, Injuries are a part of sports, but they don't have to be a career-ending event. By taking steps to prevent injuries and having a rehabilitation plan in place, professional athletes can stay healthy and continue to perform at their best. Coaches and trainers play a critical role in helping athletes stay injury-free, and it is important for them to stay up-to-date on the latest injury prevention and rehabilitation strategies.

Career Planning and Longevity in Professional Sports

Professional athletes have a unique career trajectory that requires careful planning to ensure longevity in their sport. While talent and hard work are essential for success, it is equally important to have a long-term plan that takes into account the physical and mental demands of the sport, career goals, and potential obstacles.

Sports performance coaching plays a critical role in career planning for professional athletes. Coaches must work closely with athletes to develop personalized training programs that address their specific needs and goals. This includes building strength, improving endurance, enhancing mental toughness, and preventing injuries.

Strength and conditioning coaching for athletes should focus on developing functional strength that translates to on-field performance. This includes exercises that improve power, explosiveness, and agility while also reducing the risk of injury. Endurance training coaching for runners and cyclists should focus on developing the energy systems needed for sustained performance over long distances.

Mental performance coaching for competitive sports is crucial for helping athletes maintain focus, manage stress, and develop the resilience needed to overcome setbacks. Nutrition coaching for athletes is also essential for optimizing performance and recovery. This includes developing a balanced diet that provides the necessary nutrients for optimal performance, as well as strategies for fueling before, during, and after competition. Injury prevention and rehabilitation coaching for athletes is critical for minimizing the risk of injury and ensuring a speedy recovery in the event of an injury. This includes developing injury prevention strategies, incorporating injury prevention exercises into training programs, and working closely with medical professionals to develop rehabilitation programs.

Speed and agility training coaching for athletes should focus on developing the technical skills needed for optimal performance. This includes drills that improve footwork, change of direction, and acceleration. Sports-specific coaching for football, basketball, soccer, and other sports should focus on developing the skills and tactics needed for success in each sport. Youth sports performance coaching for young athletes should focus on developing a foundation of skills and habits that will help them succeed in their sport and develop a love of physical activity. Post-collegiate sports performance coaching for professional athletes should focus on developing a long-term career plan that takes into account their unique talents and goals. Finally, recovery and regeneration coaching for athletes is essential for ensuring that athletes can train and compete at their best. This includes developing recovery strategies that incorporate rest, sleep, and nutrition, as well as incorporating regeneration exercises into training programs.

Conclusion

Career planning and longevity in professional sports require a comprehensive approach that takes into account the physical and mental demands of the sport, career goals, and potential obstacles. Sports performance coaches play a critical role in helping athletes develop personalized training programs that address their specific needs and goals, as well as strategies for injury prevention, mental toughness, nutrition, and recovery. By taking a comprehensive approach to career planning, athletes can maximize their potential and achieve long-term success in their sport.

Chapter 15: Recovery and Regeneration Coaching for Athletes

Importance of Recovery and Regeneration

As a coach or movement specialist, you must understand that training and practice are essential components of an athlete's success. However, what many coaches fail to realize is that recovery and regeneration are equally as important. Athletes who do not prioritize recovery and regeneration are more prone to injuries, burnout, and decreased performance levels. Therefore, it is essential to understand the importance of recovery and regeneration in sports-specific coaching.

Recovery refers to the time an athlete takes to rest and repair their body after an intense training session or competition. This is when the body adapts to the stress of exercise, allowing the athlete to come back stronger and perform better in the future. On the other hand, regeneration refers to the active processes that athletes undertake to speed up the recovery process, such as foam rolling, stretching, massage, and other techniques.

One of the most significant benefits of recovery and regeneration is injury prevention. When an athlete's body is not given enough time to recover properly, it becomes more vulnerable to injuries. Over time, this can lead to chronic injuries that can negatively impact an athlete's career. By prioritizing recovery and regeneration, coaches can help their athletes avoid these injuries and stay healthy.

Another benefit of recovery and regeneration is improved performance. When an athlete's body is allowed to recover fully, they can perform at their best during training sessions and competitions. In contrast, athletes who do not prioritize recovery and regeneration may experience decreased performance levels due to fatigue, soreness, and other factors.

Recovery refers to the time an athlete takes to rest and repair their body after an intense training session or competition. This is when the body adapts to the stress.

In addition to injury prevention and improved performance, recovery and regeneration can also have mental health benefits. Athletes who take the time to recover and regenerate their bodies are more likely to experience reduced stress levels and increased mental clarity. This can help them stay focused and motivated, enabling them to perform at their best.

As a coach or movement specialist, it is essential to prioritize recovery and regeneration in your training programs. By doing so, you can help your athletes avoid injuries, improve their performance, and maintain their mental health. Remember that recovery and regeneration are just as important as training and practice when it comes to unlocking an athlete's full potential.

Techniques for Recovery and Regeneration

As a coach or movement specialist, one of your key responsibilities is ensuring that your athletes are able to recover and regenerate effectively. This is critical for preventing injuries and improving performance over the long term. In this section, we will explore some of the most effective techniques for recovery and regeneration, including nutrition, sleep, stretching, and more.

Nutrition is perhaps the most important factor when it comes to recovery and regeneration. Athletes need to consume a balanced diet that is rich in protein, carbohydrates, and healthy fats. They also need to stay hydrated by drinking plenty of water and electrolyte-rich fluids. It's important to work with a nutrition coach or specialist to develop a customized nutrition plan that meets the specific needs of each athlete. Sleep is another critical factor in recovery and regeneration. Athletes need to get enough sleep each night to allow their bodies to repair and rebuild muscles and tissues. Most athletes need at least 8 hours of sleep each night, although some may require more. Coaches should work with athletes to establish good sleep habits, such as sticking to a regular sleep schedule and creating a sleep-conducive environment. Stretching is also an important technique for recovery and regeneration. Athletes should stretch before and after each workout to help reduce the risk of injury and improve flexibility. Dynamic stretching before a workout can help prepare the muscles for exercise, while static stretching after a workout can help reduce muscle soreness and promote recovery.

Massage and foam rolling are other effective recovery techniques. Massage can help improve circulation, reduce muscle tension, and promote relaxation. Foam rolling can help release trigger points and knots in the muscles, which can help reduce muscle soreness and improve flexibility.

Finally, coaches should encourage their athletes to take rest days and to listen to their bodies. Overtraining can lead to fatigue, injury, and burnout, so it's important to give the body time to recover between workouts. By incorporating these techniques into your coaching strategy, you can help your athletes recover and regenerate effectively, which can lead to improved performance and a reduced risk of injury over the long term.

Sleep and Rest for Athletic Performance

One of the most overlooked aspects of athletic performance is sleep and rest. As a coach, it is important to educate your athletes about the importance of sleep, and to encourage them to prioritize rest and recovery as part of their training regimen.

Sleep is essential for athletic performance because it is during sleep that the body repairs and regenerates itself. Athletes who do not get enough sleep are more prone to injuries, suffer from decreased reaction time, and have a reduced ability to concentrate. Additionally, sleep deprivation can lead to a decrease in performance and an increase in fatigue.

To optimize athletic performance, athletes should aim for at least 7-9 hours of sleep per night. However, the quality of sleep is just as important as the quantity. Athletes should strive to create a sleep environment that is conducive to restful sleep, such as keeping the bedroom cool and dark, avoiding electronic devices before bedtime, and establishing a consistent sleep routine.

Rest and recovery are also important components of athletic performance. Athletes who train intensely and frequently need time to recover and allow their bodies to adapt to the stress of training. This can be achieved through active recovery, such as stretching, foam rolling, and light exercise, as well as passive recovery, such as massage and rest days.

As a coach, it is important to monitor your athletes' sleep and recovery habits and to make adjustments to their training regimen as needed. Encouraging your athletes to prioritize sleep and rest will improve not only their athletic performance but also their overall health and well-being.

In conclusion, sleep and rest are crucial components of athletic performance that should not be overlooked. As coaches, we have a responsibility to educate our athletes about the importance of sleep and to encourage them to prioritize rest and recovery as part of their training regimen. By doing so, we can help our athletes unlock their full potential and achieve their goals both on and off the field.

Mindfulness and Mental Recovery Techniques

As a movement specialist or coach, your focus is not only on physical training but also on mental strategies that can help athletes unlock their potential and reach peak performance. Mindfulness and mental recovery techniques are essential tools that can help athletes manage stress, reduce anxiety, and improve their mental focus. These techniques can be particularly useful in sports that require high levels of concentration, such as football, basketball, and soccer.

Mindfulness is the practice of being present and fully engaged in the moment, without judgment or distraction. This technique can help athletes stay focused and calm under pressure, which is critical for success in competitive sports. Mindfulness can also help athletes stay in tune with their bodies, which can help prevent injuries and improve recovery time.

Mental recovery techniques can also help athletes manage stress and recover from intense training sessions and competitions. These techniques can include meditation, visualization, and deep breathing exercises. Meditation can help athletes clear their minds and reduce stress, while visualization can help them mentally rehearse their performances and build confidence. Deep breathing exercises can help athletes regulate their breathing and calm their nervous system, which can help improve their mental focus.

When coaching athletes, it is important to incorporate mindfulness and mental recovery techniques into their training programs. By teaching athletes how to manage stress and improve their mental focus, coaches can help them reach their full potential and achieve their goals. It is important to note that these techniques are not just for athletes who are struggling with mental health issues; they can benefit all athletes, regardless of their mental state. In conclusion, mindfulness and mental recovery techniques are essential tools for coaches and movement specialists who work with athletes. By incorporating these techniques into training programs, coaches can help athletes manage stress, improve mental focus, and unlock their potential. These techniques are particularly important for athletes in high-pressure sports, but they can benefit all athletes, regardless of their sport or level of competition.

Chapter 16: How to improve your players' Performance in 15 minutes?

The SPT (Speed Performance Training) Routine minimizes unnecessary movements. SPT focuses on the quality of the quantity movement that is significant to preparation and development. Athletes must have speed, quickness, and agility to perform at a high level for events and competitions. Over the last 25 years, every player I worked with wanted to increase their speed, so I've spent a significant amount of time developing The SPT routine that could get your players better in 15 minutes. When coaches say they need specific players, he's looking for a specific skill set. I've developed this SPT (Speed Performance Training) system to accommodate every coach's wish list. The Northstar SPT routine utilizes Analytics, technique, and performance-based drills to increase productivity. Coaches must understand how to develop physical skill sets.

My motto is **"To Build a solid foundation for the future in movement!"**

Sports is a game of speed, strength, explosiveness, and elite skill set. I've seen speed impact a game in more ways than I can count. I've seen many coaches struggle with developing a Speed Performance program, so we are here to make your job easier. SPT is a customized program designed to help athletes and teams. Through years of research, I have customized the SPT program that increases individual athlete efficiency and their opportunities for success. I have identified several skill sets that are important to skill enhancement. Now, I'm ready to give out these insider secrets to help develop Championship programs and injury-free seasons. SPT can help players develop explosive speed and lightning quickness with performance warm-ups. From a coach's perspective, this also provides a framework for what we need to assess and monitor to put our players in a better position for success.

Typical warm-up routines do not reflect speed, so I have designed the following SPT warm-up routine to incorporate speed into individual and team warm-up routines. In a performance warm-up routine, I have defined the conditions of the circuit to ensure it is safe and meets the overall objectives of the warm-up.

Important Note: Before trying this out with your athletes, be sure to have them jog and skip for about five minutes.

Speed Practice Training and Warm-up Routine

This book will break down how to utilize different communication techniques in your training process and evaluate players. Also, some of the methods I use in these drills will be called partial learning. Then, we will set them on a complex training course so they will be put together piece by piece from the first step you would take until the last step you take. These drills are all related to partial learning. When you are warming up, the exercises should be partially learning, so do not overlook the warm-up drills. They must be done and partial learning so that once you hit the fill, your mind and your body have already gone through the movements. To be a high-level coach, you must communicate well with your players to succeed. Sharing is essential, so we will go through some of the drills and talk about the techniques we've utilized to develop players from partial learning to complex high-level movements.

Here's a warm-up routine to build up total performance. Jogging a lap and skipping halfway is significant in learning how to warm up the lower legs and get more dorsiflexion. It also strengthens the ankles, which control the body, increasing speed and coordination. The jog should be a rhythm run, and players should be running on the balls of their feet, not flat-footed, which will also help increase the dynamic balance in the lower legs.

Technical Drills for Running

Technical drills for runners are usually performed using four activities: marching, lateral shuffle(walking), skipping, and running. Each exercise helps to develop essential components of proper and economical running techniques.

There are several reasons for using the activities. These exercises serve as an excellent warm-up tool for training and competitive situations. Running drills should imitate specific characteristics of technically proper running form, including an upright posture of the trunk and spinal column, good carriage of the arms during the running stride, appropriate knee drive and leg action, and the coordinated dynamic balance associated with shifting weight from one leg to the other.

These drills help develop the essential proprioceptive and kinaesthetic (body awareness) abilities that a runner must have to deal with changes in direction while running and to 'change gears' during games. The drills are performed slowly at first while developing a 'feel' for proper technique. A sound strategy is then gradually carried over to exercises and runs at faster speeds. The exercises also help strengthen specific muscle groups needed for powerful running, especially the feet, calves, shins, thighs, and hips. The ankle, knee, and hip joints undergo considerable flexion and extension during the running stride. Each of these joints is exercised through a similar or more excellent range of motion during the various drills.

Walking through high knees

The fundamentals must be done correctly. Walk through slowly, stop on each step, and check the knee and arm position.

Lateral shuffle walk.

This also is a technical drill and a strengthening drill. Two techniques on one exercise, shuffling your feet and keeping your feet apart shoulder-width, keeping your center of gravity low and chest up; also, this serves as a strengthening drill and starts to train your CNC nervous system to be balanced.

Caraoka walk

This is a very important drill that produces athleticism and strengthens the hips by stretching the hips. The technique is essential that you cross the legs over and drop the back knee down to the ground in a lunge position. Repeat on the other side from 6 to 8 times for flexibility in the hips.

Duck walk

This is an excellent way to get flexibility in your hips and also to build up strength and coordination. The following drills are done when stationary:

Bouncing on toes

Small, quick bounces of the ankle to get the dorsiflex moving.

Bounce on toes for height

This builds up explosive power (dynamic balance) in the lower extremity.

Running on a spot

These are stationary drills, but they also help produce rhythm with the feet and the critical arms. It helps increase the dorsal flexion in the knee and the hip joint. Coaching Point players must be light on their feet and in rhythm when running on a spot.

All of the following drills are done 10-20 yards before an event or competition takes place.

Bunny hops

This drill is a critical component to performance; the feet are the only thing that has contact with the ground and must be warmed up and strengthened to be efficient. This component increases your Performance and your reaction speed.

Toe-tapping

This is the same as running on a spot, but it is moving. The player is moving forward with quick feet.

Coaching Point: the player must be light on his feet, moving forward as fast as possible, arms pumping with no Facial expressions, and staying relaxed while doing all drills, which also creates rhythm.

High Knees in Place

Athletes will accelerate their arm speed for 10 seconds. This is one of the new concepts that have been around for years. Players do high knees and concentrate on the rhythm of movement, staying light on their feet and accelerating their arms. This drill also increases your acceleration speed in a stationary position.

This is memorized in their central nervous system and can now be transferred to the field or court.

Medium-high knees at half speed

You must concentrate on good technique and rhythm. The player must stay light on their feet, stay in their arm pump, and keep in rhythm with their arms and feet. This drill is critical for the rhythm of movement, whether individually or in a team. This drill will increase the rhythm of the movement of your athletes.

High knees with fast arm swings

(Driving of the elbow back is key to explosive

speed.) This is one of my favorite drills to increase speed. The player starts with high knees in place.

The player must be given a mental suggestion to speed up the arms. The player will notice that their legs will go faster. Because of the arms, they will understand the concept of acceleration. Your arms are your engine, and your legs are wheels. If you try to accelerate with your wheels and do not use your arms, there will be an imbalance in the rhythm and power you are trying to produce. The body is a unit; it works together, so the arms are controlled by the central nervous system, which controls the reactionary speed that controls the legs. I have seen this on several occasions as I have done my research. Oftentimes, athletes with long arm swings are in panic mode and cannot accelerate. A player does not feel the acceleration speed that they normally feel. Therefore, coaches tell them to keep pumping their arms because they lose their speed when they stop pumping their arms.

High Knee Sprint

This is one of the most important drills you can do if you are an athlete who wants explosive speed and lightning quickness. One of the things you must understand about being explosive and accelerating quickly is how much force you can create toward the ground and how light you can stay on your feet, resulting in explosive speed and quickness. This is one of the most overlooked drills that I have seen from several teams that I have surveyed. The whole team does high knees, and then everyone has their own unique program that they are working on. Then, your team has different results when it gets on the field. Each player must have the same information on the important things that will lead to success on the field or court. This is one of the critical things that I have found in athletes that are lacking the ability to pick their knees up and put their feet into the ground.

Running backward

Take long strides while leaning forward with all the weight on your front foot and ankle to help increase dynamic balance. This is critical to increasing speed and performance as it Increases your forward lean. It also increases your balance when using forward lean and your strength with the total body weight pushing and reaching back. It's more of an explosive plyometric drill backward. These are all things that are possible to increase performance while doing your warm-up routine. The most crucial part of this program is that the player understands what they are accomplishing with their drill; this is a downhill running drill in reverse and the key to staying light on feet and staying in your arms pump.

Quick Caraoka

You must be standing upright, working the hips, and moving your feet quickly. Use quick Caraoka drills, develop your footwork, and increase the rotation of your hips to increase your lateral quickness. This one drill will improve footwork and reaction speed. All players must be light on their feet, keeping a base and staying under control, which can be done in a quick motion after players learn motions. You should speed up the drill for max results.

Caraoka (Bent knees leverage position)

Another important drill when trying to develop athletes or select an athlete is the ability to move hips and feet when in a low center of gravity. If you engage with another athlete, you also have to be able to turn and run with smoothness and speed when in a low center of gravity. Most players do not play with a low center of gravity, but this is critical to increasing athletic performance.

Side stride Caraoka (Heisman Trophy)

One of the most critical parts of the Caraoka drill is the hip movement. This is the reason you change directions; it is the back hip rotation in the direction you are going; your front foot sets the direction, and the back foot moves your body in that direction. This is something that you see on a Heisman Trophy; it is the movement of a superior athlete, and everyone I've seen in the last few years does this drill wrong. Mobility drills for the hips increase the angles of efficiency when moving laterally. Pick the knee up to hip height, rotating the hips in the opposite direction, and get your feet back underneath and balanced. Repeat this drill ten times in one direction and concentrate on being light on your feet.

Caraoka & Sprint (Transitional Movement)

Flip your back hip, be explosive on that first stride, and understand how to use body lean to increase the downhill running out of your break. This pose is on the Heisman trophy, and it represents a great athletic movement. Understanding how to use body lean to increase performance in this drill is important.

This drill is what I call a transitional drill, where you come from one drill and transition into another drill. This is a critical component to developing defensive and offensive players that have good hip movement and can run, so this drill is very critical to teaching you how to move and sprint.

Speed acceleration

As discussed earlier, speed acceleration in this portion is about using the Valsalva technique of raising your blood pressure to increase your speed.

Starting speed

When talking about starting speed, the most common mistake is a false step, overstriding, or trying too hard. I've used the illustration of a car starting in third gear that stalls out, so the player understands you must take smaller steps in initiating the movement and slowly increase the stride through the force produced from the knee action to the ground until it gets into a natural stride. When starting from a stationary position, the player must take quick steps utilizing the forward lane in the direction before applying force or torque.

Acceleration speed

This is another important drill when recruiting guys with explosive power. This is called the Valsalva technique. This drill is one of the reasons why track does not help increase explosive power.

Deceleration

Deceleration has a lot to do with changing directions. So, this is a critical drill to practice for balance techniques and reaction speed. Players must run for 5, 10, and 20 yards. Decelerate, come under control and check their feet to see if they're in a balanced position. The key is to be light on your feet and relax when breaking down.

Re-acceleration speed

Players must have the ability to stop their feet and re-accelerate. This is critical because sports is about changing directions and reaccelerating; it must be trained in the central nervous system.

Acceleration technique

The Valsalva technique is an essential technique; it is a natural technique for the human body. Everybody can use the Valsalva technique to understand how to raise their blood pressure to increase the strength or performance that they need for that task, so the Valsalva technique is one of the most important things a player playing any sport can have. It is one of the characteristics of very successful players to be able to move quickly. Being quicker than your opponent means that you have an advantage in speed. I believe you need to pay a lot of attention to acceleration drills.

This can be done in several different ways, but if you are interested in changing your player's skill set to an explosive skill set, then you would need to practice this drill in training and have the player do his own workouts on this type of drill. The players will jog 5 yards and sprint hard for 10 to 20 yards; after that, the players will sprint at 3/4th speed yards and accelerate hard for 20 yards.

Acceleration and Breakdown

I like to use these drills: under control running, Caraoka, shuffling, backpaddling acceleration for 10-20-30 yards, and breaking down; this helps the body control transitional movement, balance, and coordination, which helps reduce injuries. It is about staying under control, getting small, and staying light on your feet. Make sure to make the players sprint, stop, and check their feet to see if they're balanced.

Reaction speed

Reaction speed is the interval time between the presence of a stimulus and the initiation of a muscle response to that stimulus. A primary factor affecting the response is the number of possible stimuli, each of which requires a response. If there is only one response, simple reaction time, it will only take a short time to react. If there are several possibilities for response time choice reaction time, then it will take longer to determine which response to carry out. It's very simple to increase your reaction speed using a whistle; it is much simpler and trains the same part of the brain.

Change of Direction Play

Athletes will run 5 yards squared up in a defensive position or ready position and push, drive, and stride in the other direction. This should be repeated at least 5 to 10 times, depending on the player's level of understanding. A pivotal element of sports is that players must be more athletic and change direction without losing speed. This drill can teach players how to defend and increase reaction speed in space by utilizing a whistle. This should eliminate poor reaction speed.

The player should be dropping his hips and lowering his center of gravity whenever changing directions. This is critical, and coaches should check to see if the player's feet are balanced when he decides to change directions.

Change of Direction

This drill is a 180-degree turn. Players should use the balance concept when getting in and out of their breaks. This drill could be done as a team, but it should be done for at least 10 to 15 seconds at 75%. Also, it can be utilized for a PT workout after practice conditioning.

Circle cuts (center field turn)

The athlete should never be stopping their feet; you come from a stride position into a small stride position that is more balanced with quick feet, keeping your feet underneath you until you can get back into an accelerated stride phase. Doing it too soon will result in injury or failure to execute the play.

Full-circle cuts could be large or small circles, but both must be trained in your warm-up routine and training. A half-circle cut is a change of direction circle cut where the player can reverse their position without stopping their feet. A 1/4 circle cut is a speed cut.

Drill: Place cones 5 yards apart from the player so he can run around. The cone players must be as close to the cone as possible and sprint out with high knee action.

Nebraska drill

This drill has two essential components to cutting: a circle cut or a plant cut. This must be trained in partial learning technique, so the player must understand the concept of toe-tapping with small steps for circular cuts and planting driving for angular cuts. Acceleration speed: understanding how to get control of your body. Using the toe-tapping method around the cone, keep your feet close to the ground. Get out of your break with a high knee sprint, break your feet back down to a small quick step, and then accelerate out to full speed again.

Angular cuts

These cuts are planting and driving out of your brakes. Use a 45-degree angle in the opposite direction, break your feet down, and get in and out of your break.

Four Cones Drill

Start by getting your feet balanced and in a ready position to react. Make a right or left turn and be in a good reactionary position. Here is how to utilize partial learning with one drill that can be utilized to learn several different parts of sports performance. In all of these drills I have just gone over, we must use analytics, and you must time players at these drills to find out how your players respond under pressure. The next thing is to take a whistle or ball out and utilize these drills. Develop game reaction speed, which is critical to developing good athletes and having great reaction time.

Conclusion

Here is how to utilize partial learning with one drill that can be utilized to learn several different parts of sports performance.

Sports-specific coaching costs about $450, a movement specialist certification, video conferences, and phone conferences. Your athletes will be loose, agile, and fast—in fact, utilizing SPT warm-ups is the only way to do it if you want a championship team with a minimum of injuries. When you incorporate Performance warm-ups into your training method, you can expect an immediate improvement in the success of the athletes you work with.

The magic of coordination and rhythm coordination is the ability to repeatedly execute a sequence of movements smoothly and accurately. This may involve the senses, muscular contractions, and joint movements. The word 'coordinated' is defined as the ability to use more than one set of muscle movements to a single end. Everything we participate in requires the ability to coordinate our limbs to achieve a successful outcome—from walking to the more complex movements of athletics. The rhythm of movement is fundamental to both movement and rhythm.

Include the basic movement techniques designed to give the athlete an understanding of body alignment, body balance, and control of the center.

Chapter 17: Summary of Key Points

This book is filled with a wealth of knowledge and expertise that will benefit any coach or movement specialist working with athletes. In this chapter, we will summarize the key points discussed throughout the book.

Firstly, it is crucial to understand the importance of sports-specific coaching. Each sport requires different skills, movements, and physical attributes that athletes must develop to perform at an elite level. Therefore, coaches must have a deep understanding of the sport they are coaching and tailor their approach to meet the unique needs of their athletes.

Secondly, strength and conditioning coaching for athletes is an essential component of sports-specific coaching. Coaches must develop training programs that focus on building strength, power, speed, and agility while also addressing any weaknesses or imbalances in an athlete's body. Furthermore, endurance training coaching for runners and cyclists is equally important, as it enables athletes to maintain their performance levels for extended periods.

Thirdly, mental performance coaching for competitive sports is a key aspect of sports-specific coaching that is often overlooked. Coaches must help athletes develop mental toughness, focus, and resilience to perform at their best under pressure.

Fourthly, nutrition coaching for athletes is crucial for optimal performance. Coaches must educate athletes on the importance of proper nutrition and develop meal plans that meet their unique needs.

Fifthly, injury prevention and rehabilitation coaching for athletes is essential to keep athletes healthy and performing at their best. Coaches must develop injury prevention strategies and work closely with sports medicine professionals to ensure any injuries are treated effectively.

Sixthly, speed and agility training coaching for athletes is vital to help athletes develop the explosive movements required for their sport. Coaches must develop programs that focus on improving an athlete's first-step quickness, acceleration, and deceleration.

Seventhly, youth sports performance coaching for young athletes is vital, as it sets the foundation for their future success in sports. Coaches must prioritize proper technique and development over winning at all costs. Eighthly, post-collegiate sports performance coaching for professional athletes is essential to help athletes maintain their performance levels and prevent injuries as they age. Coaches must develop programs that focus on recovery, regeneration, and injury prevention. Finally, recovery and regeneration coaching for athletes is critical to help athletes recover from intense training sessions and prevent burnout. Coaches must implement recovery strategies such as proper sleep, nutrition, and rest days to ensure athletes are healthy and performing at their best.

In conclusion, Sports-Specific Coaching for Elite Athletes: Unlocking Potential in Football, Basketball, Soccer, and More, provides coaches and movement specialists with a comprehensive guide to developing athletes' full potential. By prioritizing sports-specific coaching, strength and conditioning, mental performance, nutrition, injury prevention, speed and agility training, youth and post-collegiate coaching, and recovery and regeneration, coaches can help athletes perform at their best and achieve their full potential.

Importance of Sports-Specific Coaching

Sports-specific coaching is a crucial component of the development of elite athletes. While general coaching can provide athletes with a solid foundation of knowledge and skills, sports-specific coaching enables athletes to refine their technique and improve their performance in their specific sport. This explores the importance of sports-specific coaching for various niches of sports performance coaching, including strength and conditioning coaching, endurance training coaching, mental performance coaching, nutrition coaching, injury prevention and rehabilitation coaching, speed, and agility training coaching, sports-specific coaching for football, basketball, soccer, and more, youth sports performance coaching, post-collegiate sports performance coaching, and recovery and regeneration coaching.

Strength and conditioning coaching for athletes can benefit greatly from sports-specific coaching. By focusing on the specific demands of an athlete's sport, coaches can design training programs that will improve their strength, power, and explosiveness in ways that will directly translate to their performance on the field or court. Endurance training coaching can also benefit from sports-specific coaching, as coaches can tailor their programs to the specific energy demands of the athlete's sport, helping them to improve their stamina and endurance.

Mental performance coaching is another area where sports-specific coaching can be of great benefit. By working with athletes to develop mental skills such as focus, confidence, and resilience that are specific to their sport, coaches can help athletes to perform at their best under pressure. Nutrition coaching can also benefit from sports-specific coaching, as coaches can help athletes to tailor their diets to the specific demands of their sport, ensuring that they are getting the nutrients they need to perform at their best.

Injury prevention and rehabilitation coaching is another area where sports-specific coaching can be of great benefit. By focusing on the specific demands of an athlete's sport, coaches can design programs that target areas of the body that are particularly prone to injury, helping athletes to avoid or recover from injuries more quickly. Speed and agility training coaching can also benefit from sports-specific coaching, as coaches can design programs that improve an athlete's ability to move quickly and change direction in ways that are specific to their sport.

Sports-specific coaching for football, basketball, soccer, and other sports is essential for athletes who want to reach their full potential. By focusing on the specific skills and techniques that are required in each sport, coaches can help athletes to refine their technique and improve their performance in ways that will directly translate to their success on the field or court. Youth sports performance coaching and post-collegiate sports performance coaching can also benefit from sports-specific coaching, as coaches can help athletes to develop the skills they need to compete at the next level.

Finally, recovery and regeneration coaching is another area where sports-specific coaching can be of great benefit. By focusing on the specific demands of an athlete's sport, coaches can design recovery programs that help athletes to recover more quickly and effectively from their workouts and competitions, allowing them to perform at their best over the long term.

In conclusion, sports-specific coaching is essential for athletes who want to reach their full potential. By focusing on the specific demands of an athlete's sport, coaches can help athletes to refine their technique, improve their performance, and avoid injuries, all of which are essential for success at the elite level. Whether you are a strength and conditioning coach, an endurance training coach, a mental performance coach, a nutrition coach, an injury prevention and rehabilitation coach, a speed and agility training coach, or a sports-specific coach for football, basketball, soccer, or other sports, sports-specific coaching should be an essential part of your coaching toolkit.

Next Steps for Athletes and Coaches

As an athlete or coach, you have likely spent countless hours training, practicing, and competing. But what comes next? How can you continue to improve and reach your full potential? Here are some next steps to consider:

1. **Set Goals**: Whether you are an athlete or a coach, setting goals is crucial for success. Goals help provide direction and motivation. Make sure your goals are specific, measurable, achievable, relevant, and time-bound (SMART). Also, make sure to revisit your goals periodically and adjust them as needed.

2. **Seek Feedback**: Feedback is essential for growth. As an athlete or coach, seek feedback from peers, mentors, and experts. Listen to constructive criticism and use it to improve your skills and performance.

3. **Continue Learning**: The world of sports is constantly evolving. As an athlete or coach, it is important to stay up-to-date with the latest research, trends, and best practices. Attend seminars, conferences, and workshops. Read books and articles. Take online courses. Continuously learn and refine your skills.

4. **Prioritize Recovery:** Recovery is just as important as training. As an athlete or coach, make sure to prioritize recovery. This includes proper nutrition, hydration, sleep, and rest. Also, consider incorporating techniques such as foam rolling, stretching, and massage to aid in recovery and prevent injuries.

5. **Embrace Mental Training**: Sports are not just physical. Mental strength and toughness are also critical for success. As an athlete or coach, consider

incorporating mental training techniques such as visualization, mindfulness, and positive self-talk. Also, seek the help of a mental performance coach if needed.

6. Foster Positive Relationships: Success in sports is not just about individual performance. It also involves teamwork, communication, and positive relationships. As an athlete or coach, foster positive relationships with teammates, coaches, and support staff. Also, consider giving back to the community through volunteer work and mentorship.

In conclusion, as an athlete or coach, the journey to success never ends. Set goals, seek feedback, continue learning, prioritize recovery, embrace mental training, and foster positive relationships. These next steps will help you unlock your full potential and achieve success in sports and beyond.

Made in the USA
Coppell, TX
20 June 2026

82554782R00105